# Rent Seeking and Human Capital



*Rent Seeking and Human Capital: How the Hunt for Rents Is Changing Our Economic and Political Landscape* explores the debates around rent seeking and contextualizes it within the capitalist economy.

It is vital that the field of economics does a better job of analyzing and making policy recommendations that reduce the opportunities and rewards for rent seeking, generating returns from the redistribution of wealth rather than wealth creation. This short and provocative book addresses the key questions: Who are the rent seekers? What do they do? Where do they come from? What are the consequences of rent seeking for the broader economy? And, finally: What should policymakers do about them? The chapters examine the existing literature on rent seeking, including looking at the differences between rent seeking and economic rent. The work provides an in-depth look at the case of the impact of rent seeking degrees in the United States, particularly in business and law, and explores potential policy remedies, such as a wealth tax, changes to the rules on financial transactions, and patent law reform.

This text provides an important intervention on rent seeking for students and scholars of heterodox economics, political economy, inequality, and anyone interested in the shape of the modern capitalist economy.

**Kurt von Seekamm Jr.** is Assistant Professor in the Department of Economics at Salem State University, USA.

## Routledge Frontiers of Political Economy



For more information about this series, please visit: www.routledge.com/books/series/SE0345

# Rent Seeking and Human Capital

## How the Hunt for Rents Is Changing Our Economic and Political Landscape

**Kurt von Seekamm Jr.**

Routledge
Taylor & Francis Group
LONDON AND NEW YORK

First published 2021
by Routledge
2 Park Square, Milton Park, Abingdon, Oxon OX14 4RN

and by Routledge
605 Third Avenue, New York, NY 10017

*Routledge is an imprint of the Taylor & Francis Group, an informa business*



*British Library Cataloguing-in-Publication Data*
A catalogue record for this book is available from the British Library

*Library of Congress Cataloging-in-Publication Data*
A catalog record for this book has been requested

ISBN 13: 978-0-367-34992-9 (hbk)
ISBN 13: 978-0-367-62297-8 (pbk)

Typeset in Times New Roman
by Apex CoVantage, LLC

# Contents

# Acknowledgments

I would like to thank all of those that made the writing of this book possible. In particular, I'm appreciative to the Faculty Writing Group and the Center for Research and Creative Activities at Salem State University for providing space to write and resources for this project. I am also grateful to Travis Keon for providing insightful comments. Finally, a very special thank you to my wife, Katherine, for her comments, edits, and unwavering love and support.

# 1 A primer on inequality

Drive far enough on a snowy, tree-lined road in the middle of nowhere Montana and you will encounter a stand-alone stone building occupied by security guards. If you're lucky enough to be on the guest list or, even luckier, a member, a quick ID check is all you need to gain access to perhaps the most exclusive private ski resort in the world, the famed Yellowstone Club in Big Sky, Montana.

For ski enthusiasts, treatment at the Yellowstone Club feels different than at non-membership ski resorts. There are no long walks hauling gear from distant parking lots. Instead, a valet meets you at the entrance to an opulent clubhouse to park your car and shepherd your skis slope-side. Crowded and overpriced food courts packed with bags and people struggling to put on their ski gear are replaced by a clubhouse with a complimentary barista and hot breakfast, including fare like "pigs in a parka" and acai bowls. Long lift lines on powder days are replaced by nearly entirely empty chairlifts, ensuring that untouched lines exist well past the next snowfall.

Such is life for the 800-plus[1] very rich and variably famous members. And to be clear, members are indeed very rich. With an initiation fee of $300,000, annual dues of $41,500 per year, and a requirement to own property at the resort ranging from just under $3 million for undeveloped land to tens of millions of dollars for lavish mansions, all but the most well-off are kept off the membership roster.[2]

For the uninitiated, it seems unfathomable as to why, or perhaps even how, such a place could exist. At a time when 39% of American households cannot pay a surprise $400 expense without selling assets or taking on new debt and 25% of adults skipped necessary medical treatment due to their inability to pay, the divide between the average American and the superrich American is all the more telling.[3] However, Americans' attitudes about the level of inequality are mixed. The trend in the number of Americans who think that the government should intervene and reduce the level of income differences has been virtually unchanged since 1978 even as income differences have skyrocketed.[4]

The dramatic increase in income inequality is well documented by economists. Indeed, the seminal work by Thomas Piketty and Emmanuel Saez, "Income Inequality in the United States, 1913–1998", sparked debates among politicians and economists alike, led to the publication of countless papers and books on the subject, and prompted the collection and sharing of global income data through the World Incomes Database.

Within this debate, there has been a tendency to treat income inequality as a moral issue with normative statements abound. More liberal outlets such as the *Washington Post* and the *New York Times* describe income inequality as "How Income Inequality Hurts America"[5] and "Income Inequality: It's Also Bad for Your Health"[6] while more conservative outlets describe income inequality as "The Inequality Delusion: Why We've Got the Wealth Gap All Wrong"[7] and "Income Inequality Is Good for the Poor".[8]

So why such a dramatic divide? Ideology certainly plays a role. For conservatives, income is unequivocally viewed as a reward to good decisions made by the recipients. The rewarded are people who worked hard, earned their way into good schools, worked hard, earned job offers at good companies, worked hard, and advanced up the ranks based on their merit. Liberals, however, have a different view of how the rich end up at the top of the income ladder, through a combination of luck, fraud, structural advantages, and preferential treatment by those in power, oftentimes, the already-established rich.

However, the reality is likely somewhere between the two. The "pull yourself up by your bootstraps" stories of success are oversimplified, and the "cheat your way to the top" descriptions are mostly incomplete. Even worse, in the current climate of blind bipartisanship in the United States, it seems that very few have actually taken the time to look beyond the headlines to try to unpack exactly what makes inequality good or bad and what, if anything, we can or even should do about it.

Fortunately, a more nuanced approach to thinking about inequality can help untangle the good from the bad and inform a policy approach to coping with it. In effect, that is the purpose of this book: to focus on one possible cause and result of income inequality, outline its negative consequences, and use the analysis to inform policymakers.

What is this boogeyman of income inequality? Rent seeking, the use of a resource that results in the transfer, rather than the creation, of wealth, begetting income inequality and shaping the incentives behind our education, career choices, and policies.

The remainder of this book is designed to shine a light on the concept of rent seeking. Chapter 2 gives the reader an introduction to the economic concept of rent and offers a working definition of rent seeking. Chapter 3 offers examples of where rent seeking takes place in the modern economy. Chapter 4 discusses an unexpected consequence of rent seeking, the shifting of talent, and the relationship between postsecondary degree completions by major and state-level growth in the United States. Chapter 5 discusses some of the ways politicians have tried, or perhaps failed, to address rent seeking in the US economy.

## Notes

1 Yellowstone Club Factsheet (2017, November 15). Retrieved from https://yellowstoneclub.com/wp-content/uploads/2017/11/Fact-Sheet-Dues-and-Assessments-2017-2018.pdf
2 Yellowstone Club Real Estate Guide (2018, December). Retrieved from https://yellowstoneclub.com/wp-content/uploads/2018/12/YC_Winter2018_19_REGuide_FINAL_121718.pdf
3 Federal Reserve Bank Board of Governors (2019, May). Report on the Economic Well Being of US Households. Retrieved from www.federalreserve.gov/publications/files/2018-report-economic-well-being-us-households-201905.pdf
4 Smith, Tom W., Davern, Michael, Freese, Jeremy, and Morgan, Stephen, General Social Surveys, 1972–2018 [machine-readable data file] / Principal Investigator, Smith, Tom W.; Co-Principal Investigators, Michael Davern, Jeremy Freese, and Stephen Morgan; Sponsored by National Science Foundation. –NORC ed.– Chicago: NORC, 2018: NORC at the University of Chicago [producer and distributor]. Data accessed from the GSS Data Explorer website at gssdataexplorer.norc.org.
5 Hargreaves, Steve (2013, September 25). How Income Inequality Hurts America. *CNN Business*. Retrieved from https://money.cnn.com/2013/09/25/news/economy/income-inequality
6 Sanger-Katz, Margot (2015, March 30). Income Inequality: It's Also Bad for Your Health. *The New York Times*. Retrieved from www.nytimes.com/2015/03/31/upshot/income-inequality-its-also-bad-for-your-health.html
7 Sheskin, Mark (2018, March). The Inequality Delusion: Why We've Got the Wealth Gap All Wrong. *New Scientist*. Retrieved from www.newscientist.com/article/mg23731710-300-the-inequality-delusion-why-weve-got-the-wealth-gap-all-wrong/
8 Winship, Scott (2014, November 5). Income Inequality Is Good for the Poor. *The Federalist*. Retrieved from https://thefederalist.com/2014/11/05/income-inequality-is-good-for-the-poor/

# 2 Landlords, rents, and seekers

For most, even those who have a fairly strong background in economics, the term rent brings one thing to mind, landlords. Indeed, with approximately 37%[1] of US households renting their homes, it comes as no surprise that the word rent brings to mind that pesky check you have to write at the beginning of the month. Economists use the word *rent* differently. For instance, Ricardo uses the word rent to refer to "that portion of the produce of the earth, which is paid to the landlord for the use of the original and indestructible powers of the soil".[2] In its earliest form, the term rent was originally used to describe payments to owners by users, but in its archaic economic form, it was for the use of land (by serfs), and the payment for use of the land (food) was made to the lord, hence landlord.

However, the term rent has been muddied by classical economists and modern-day economists alike. In fact, the earlier quote underlies David Ricardo's annoyance with Adam Smith's muddying of the distinction between profits and rents in the *Wealth of Nations*. Indeed, Ricardo's definition of the term rent refers to a very specific component of payments to landlords. A rent must come from the "indestructible powers of the soil". Interpreted this way, a rent is something obtained solely as a result of ownership, not business acumen, not as a result of failed markets, and certainly not as a result of any production done by the land's owner.

Adam Smith, on the other hand, uses the term rent more loosely. For Smith, a rent is at least, in part, conditional on a number of things, the location of the land, the quality of the harvest, market conditions, and so on. As such, Smith introduces a complication that Ricardo correctly identifies: rents are extremely hard to distinguish from profits. Consider his following example:

> The price of wood again varies with the state of agriculture, nearly in the same manner, and exactly for the same reason, as the price of cattle. In its rude beginnings the greater part of every country is covered with

> wood, which is then a mere encumbrance of no value to the landlord, who would gladly give it to anybody for the cutting. As agriculture advances, the woods are partly cleared by the progress of tillage, and partly go to decay in consequence of the increased number of cattle. . . . The scarcity of wood then raises its price. It affords a good rent, and the landlord sometimes finds that he can scarce employ his best lands more advantageously than in growing barren timber, of which the greatness of the profit often compensates the lateness of the returns.[3]

Simply put, rents are returns that go to the landlord, can be the result of market conditions, and can arise serendipitously to the owner.

Unlike in the Ricardian interpretation of rent, Smith opens the word up to far more liberal use that encompasses a portion of what a non-economist, or a non-interested economist, would refer to as profit. Surely, if we replace the word *landlord* with *entrepreneur* and *wood* with *intellectual property*, we could interpret income paid after expenses as a rent.

In its most basic form, a rent is a payment made after labor and other expenses used in production to some third party. In the case of agriculture, the landowner pays a farmer an income to farm the land and sell the crop. The income paid to the farmer is just enough to keep the farmer from leaving the arrangement altogether and what is left over, the rent, is paid to the landlord by virtue of owning the land. And it's this type of thinking that gives us economists' modern-day definition of a rent, "a return in excess of a resource owner's opportunity cost".[4] In layman's terms, it is income made above and beyond what is required to make the worker indifferent between participating in the market or not.

This definition brings with it a myriad of issues for distinguishing between rents and profits or even ordinary wage income. From my point of view, that's perfectly fine. In fact, rents can be paid to workers in the form of above-market wages, to shareholders who realize above-average increases in stock prices, to executives who would work for far less, and to professional athletes who, at one point, were willing to play their sport for free.

In fact, it could be argued that just about every working person in the United States receives a rent. Don't believe it? Think for a moment about your own arrangement; exactly what is the absolute lowest wage that you would bring your labor to the market? Would you leave your job to work someplace else for less? Are you indifferent between being employed or unemployed? If you are not indifferent, you're not receiving a rent. In theory, your current job pays you above your reservation wage, the wage that makes you indifferent between bringing your labor to market or living on the dole.

Economists have spent quite a bit of time and energy trying to figure out why employers pay their workers rents, wages above what they would work for, as a profit-maximizing strategy. One line of thinking behind this is that if workers are paid above their reservation wage, they will exert more effort during the workday. This increase in effort would be enough to offset the increased wage. Dubbed efficiency wage theory,[5] the justification for paying rents is to provide workers a carrot to prevent shirking, messing around on the job. Alternatively, this theory can be viewed through a labor discipline model[6] in that by paying workers a rent, the equilibrium wage is above the market-clearing wage. This ensures that there are unemployed workers in equilibrium. The existence of unemployment makes the threat to fire a worker credible and works as a stick to extract effort from workers.

There is nothing wrong with receiving a rent. Most workers do not go out into the labor market looking for them. It's a result of the firm's profit maximization strategy, but that doesn't mean that the everyday worker is aware of them. The majority of workers feel like they're underpaid, and it's unlikely that you would encounter many people who would argue that they are *overpaid.* A 2018 Gallup poll shows that while a whopping 43% of American workers feel that they are underpaid, only 5% report feeling that they are overpaid[7] even though economists would argue that many, if not all, workers receive some form of rent.

Although the average worker receives a rent, there is a wide variation in the size of the rent. For instance, unique talent or skill leads to an individual receiving high rents. As an example, professional athletes, by definition, earn very large rents. The average player in the National Basketball Association earns $6.39 million per year.[8] In Major League Baseball, it's $4.36 million,[9] and in the National Football League, it's about $2.7 million.[10] Considering that the average annual household income for Americans was $60,336 in 2017,[11] the disparity between the earnings of the average professional athlete and the average American is staggering. Much of this disparity is a result of rents.[12] Imagine what the average professional athlete would do if they never played professional sports? What would that pay? Although they receive rents, do they waste resources seeking them?

It's important to point out that rents are not reserved for workers. Firms also earn rents through market power, which is driven by a large number of factors including product differentiation, regulation, scarcity, and patents. Regardless of the source of market power, the result is that firms with market power earn monopoly rents, and those rents are proportional to the amount of market power a firm has. For instance, a firm that holds a patent for a new and innovative product has exclusive rights to produce and sell that product, giving them complete market power. This is by design, and proponents of patents argue that it's these monopoly rents that drive innovation and productivity growth.

Why does this matter? Well, for one, we need to quash this idea that rents are inherently bad or undesirable even though many seem to view them that way. By their very nature, they are simply an above-market return. They can be earned somewhat serendipitously by working in a boom industry or by design by holding a patent. Either way, in most cases, we cannot blame people, or firms, for earning rents; they are a consequence of imperfect markets.

*We can, however, blame people and firms for wasting resources seeking rents.*

In a capitalist economy, individuals and firms should, and regularly do, look to increase their income by as much as possible. One strategy to increase income would be for workers to increase their skills and productivity and for firms to innovate and invest. Another strategy would be to spend time and effort to increase the amount of income they receive without doing either. The former clearly fosters economic activity while the latter simply produces a rent and what is referred to as *rent seeking*.

Using the preceding strategies as a guide, it is possible to develop a working definition of rent seeking based on two features. First, rent seeking involves a conscious action by the rent seeker. In other words, the rent seeker intentionally uses resources specifically to capture an above-market income. Second, rent seeking is wasteful as it does not lead to an increase in productivity, innovation, or social wealth. In other words, rent seeking is the use of a resource that results in the transfer of wealth, not the creation of wealth.

The use of the term rent seeking began in earnest after papers by Tullock and Tollison. However, up until recently, the word rent seeking was reserved nearly exclusively for the lobbying of government. Consider Tullock's example of rent seeking:

> Consider a simple example in which the king wishes to grant a monopoly right in the production of playing cards. In this case, artificial scarcity is created by the state, and as a consequence, monopoly rents are present to be captured by monopolists who seek the king's favor. . . . To the extent that real resources are spent to capture monopoly rents in such ways as lobbying, these expenditures create no value from a social point of view. It is this activity of wasting resources in competing for artificially contrived transfers that is called rent seeking.[13]

And the creation of social value, benefits to the broader society that are not confined to the individual, should be the driving force of economic activity. Indeed, capitalism, under the assumptions of perfect competition, claims to maximize social welfare, the overall well-being of society.

More recently, the term rent seeking has been used far more broadly and interpreted as the pursuit of "ill-gotten gains".[14] This use of the word rent seeking opens the analysis to a far broader array of activities much in the same way Adam Smith did with his use of the word rent. Using Tullock's example, so long as there is competition for "artificially contrived transfers", rent seeking need not take place in the public sector whatsoever. Instead, the structural components of capitalism allow for rent seeking to take place and these types of activities need far more attention than economists currently give them.

## A warning

In what follows, a number of examples, possible costs, and policy prescriptions are outlined. But before moving on it should be acknowledged that rent seeking is not contrary to capitalist values. Rather, it's perfectly in line with what individuals and firms are expected to do within capitalism. Rent seeking is in our capitalist DNA. The purpose of a capitalist economy is accumulation, and obtaining rents is one of the most effective ways for individual accumulation. But the rub is this: under capitalism, accumulation is the end goal not only for the individual but also for society more generally. Rent seeking, therefore, is rational for the individual as it increases individual accumulation (individual income and firm profits increase). From a societal perspective, rent seeking is irrational as resources are wasted by being diverted away from social accumulation for the sake of individual accumulation.

This is not to say that rent seeking is morally reprehensible. In fact, under today's economic and political institutions, rent seeking is revered. So, when talking about rent seekers, the focus and energy of the critiques should not be on the individual who is doing exactly what they are supposed to do: maximizing income. Instead, the focus should be on altering the institutions that allow for the successful acquisition of rents.

It should also be noted that capitalism is not the only system under which rents occur. Indeed, readers and policymakers need to be cognizant that rents occur as a by-product of any mode of production. Critiques of unfettered capitalism, mine included, need to acknowledge that even though regulation may reduce the level of private rent seeking, a government that is willing to regulate opens the door for public rent seeking. Simply the threat of regulating an industry can lead economic agents to unleash vast troves of resources to ensure that the government does or doesn't get involved. Just take a look at much time, energy, and money the rich have put into lobbying against and evading taxes.

Without further ado, let's explore the often-overlooked world of rent seeking with some illustrative examples.

## Notes

1 Joint Center for Housing Studies of Harvard University (2018). The State of the Nation's Housing 2018. Retrieved from www.jchs.harvard.edu/sites/default/files/Harvard_JCHS_State_of_the_Nations_Housing_2018.pdf

2 Ricardo, David (1817). *On the Principles of Political Economy and Taxation.* London: John Murray, Albemarle-Street.

3 Smith, Adam (1986, First published in 1776). *The Wealth of Nations*, book I. London: Penguin Books.

4 Tollison, Robert D. (1982). Rent Seeking: A Survey. *Kyklos*, *35*(4), 575. https://doi.org/10.1111/j.1467-6435.1982.tb00174.

5 Shapiro, Carl, & Stiglitz, Joseph (1984). Equilibrium Unemployment as a Worker Discipline Device. *The American Economic Review*, *74*(3), 433.

6 Bowles, Samuel (1981). *Competitive Wage Determination and Involuntary Unemployment: A Conflict Model.* Amherst, MA: University of Massachusetts, Department of Economics. Bowles, Samuel (1985). The Production Process in a Competitive Economy: Walrasian, Neo-Hobbesian, and Marxian Models. *The American Economic Review*, *75*(1), 16–36. Retrieved from www.jstor.org/stable/1812702

7 Norman, Jim (2018, August 28). Four in 10 U.S. Workers Think They Are Underpaid. *Gallup.com*. Retrieved from https://news.gallup.com/poll/241682/four-workers-think-underpaid.aspx

8 2019–20 NBA Player Contracts | Basketball-Reference.com (n.d.). Retrieved from www.basketball-reference.com/contracts/players.html

9 MLB Average Salary 2003–2019 (n.d.). Statista. Retrieved from www.statista.com/statistics/236213/mean-salaray-of-players-in-majpr-league-baseball/

10 Klein, Gary (2018, January 26). NFL Myths: Some Players May Be "$10-million Guys," but Not All of Them Are Rich. *Los Angeles Times*. Retrieved from www.latimes.com/sports/nfl/la-sp-nfl-myths-20180126-story.html

11 Guzman, Gloria (2018, September). Household Income: 2017. *American Community Survey Briefs*. United States Census Bureau. Retrieved from www.census.gov/content/dam/Census/library/publications/2018/acs/acsbr17-01.pdf

12 It should be noted that the market is willing to pay professional athletes their staggering salaries. Great talent puts fans in the seats. Competition, fascinating storylines, and unwavering loyalty ensure that fans watch games on television, follow teams online, and buy athletes' apparel.

13 Tollison (1982).

14 Bivens, Josh, & Mishel, Lawrence (2013). The Pay of Corporate Executives and Financial Professionals as Evidence of Rents in Top 1 Percent Incomes. *Journal of Economic Perspectives*, *27*(3), 57–78. https://doi.org/10.1257/jep.27.3.57

# 3 Rent seeking

## Examples of wasted resources

### Blood, trolls, and lawyers

In 2003, 19-year-old Elizabeth Holmes filed a provisional patent for what would become US Patent Number US7291497B2 for a "[m]edical device for analyte monitoring and drug delivery". Over the next dozen years on the back of her patent, Elizabeth Holmes and the company she founded, Theranos, was able to raise $1.4 billion in funding.[1] Heralded as one of the great innovators of our time, Holmes graced the cover of magazines and won numerous accolades.

However, Theranos was a fraud. The technology that they promised, the ability to run a panel of complex blood tests using a very small amount of blood, was never made viable. The seemingly endless flow of investor money and over a decade of research and development were devoted to an idea that never came to fruition. Burdened by the prospect of failure and the intense pressure put on her by investors, Holmes ended up falsifying test results, testing blood with competitor's equipment, and lying to investors about the status of Theranos's technology.[2] The story of Elizabeth Holmes is unique in that she was able to raise so much capital and convince so many people that her idea was viable and ready for commercial use. Her story is not unique in that, in the pursuit of income, people are willing to push the boundaries of morality.

In the case of Elizabeth Holmes, it is the defrauding of investors and subsequent fruitless use of resources in pursuit of individual gains that are rent seeking. By design, patents dramatically increase the potential returns for the individual and the incentives for similar bad behavior. But this begs the question, If patents lead people to misbehave, can the pursuit of patents be labeled as rent seeking?

In the United States, the ultimate access to monopoly rents is awarded to inventors through patent protection. A US patent grants the patent holder the exclusive right to use, produce, license, or sell the intellectual property that results from an invention. The awarding of a patent offers the inventor protection from imitation by competitors. Without patent protection, a company could simply wait for an inventor to produce an innovative good and replicate it without going through the trouble or cost of inventing it. The reasons for support of patent protection should be obvious, and without patent protection, the rewards of inventing would be dramatically reduced. After all, proponents of patents argue that without the outsized rewards for your invention, all you're left with are inventions that result from the need to solve a pressing problem or the intrinsic motivation to invent.

That being said, the process of filing for a patent is not without cost. First, an inventor needs to come up with an invention that is patentable. This means that the invention has to be novel, nonobvious, adequately described or enabled, and claimed by the inventor in clear and definite terms.[3] During this process, it is normal for an inventor to hire a patent lawyer to ensure that these conditions are being met and to ensure that the patent paperwork is being filed correctly. The legal and filing fees for doing this can be in excess of $10,000.

There could be an argument that patent filings are rent seeking as the inventor seeks monopoly rents, and it uses resources (the lawyer) to acquire those monopoly rents. However, classifying patent filings as unambiguously rent seeking would be incorrect. To see why, recall the working definition of rent seeking: "the use of resources to capture above market income without increasing productivity or innovation". Since patents help foster innovation, it is impossible for them to be purely rent seeking. So should we worry about patents at all?

As it turns out, there are many opportunities to rent seek as a result of patents, not because they offer inventors monopoly rents but because they offer monopoly rents for others to capture. As a result, patents are a near-perfect case study in rent seeking because they create rents while simultaneously providing opportunities for agents to try to capture those rents.

How exactly could someone capture rents protected by patents? For one, they could try to use the legal system to invalidate an existing patent. Referred to as "patent trolls", firms that challenge valid patents are purely rent seeking. In practice, patent trolls are not actually individuals hiding under a bridge waiting for a patent holder to approach. Rather, patent trolls are sometimes referred to as nonpracticing entities, or NPEs. An NPE's sole purpose is to try to obtain licensing fees for patents as they do not conduct research and development, nor do they produce goods or services related to the patents.

NPEs, by design, seek monopoly rents granted to another firm by a patent. They do this by using vast amounts of otherwise potentially productive resources (lawyers) to try to capture those rents. As an added consequence, the holder of a valid patent wastes resources to defend their patent and monopoly rents in an attempt to stop the patent troll. The costs are not nominal; according to the American Intellectual Property Law Association's 2017 Report of the Economic Survey, the average cost for a patent infringement case is $1.7 million for each side. This nonproductive cost is a result of rent seeking. The NPE uses otherwise productive resources in the pursuit of monopoly rents and does not foster, but rather hinders, productivity growth.

Just by their existence, patent trolls have led to a proliferation of defensive NPEs referred to as "defensive aggregators".[4] Defensive aggregators are a form of NPE that buy patents from patent owners and licenses the right to use the patent back to the original owner for a fee. In return, the defensive aggregator promises to defend the patent if it is challenged in court and promises never to use the patent against the original owner. As a result, many questionable patents (ones that are likely to be litigated) find their way into defensive aggregators' patent portfolios.

With this in mind, not all patent litigation is bad. For instance, defensive aggregators, and even practicing firms for that matter, hold patents that are of questionable validity. It could be that the patent is not novel or that it is obvious as the technology was in use before filing or that it would have been discovered as a result of normal observation. In this case, the invalid patent acts as a barrier to innovation. A firm looking to use intellectual property protected by that patent should challenge that patent in court. Instead of the challenger being the rent seeker, it's the patent holder that is rent seeking by trying to block competition by obtaining a questionable patent.

As with any government intervention, a legal system that is willing to overturn patent rights and the existence of questionable patents provides fertile ground for rent seekers. This is because as soon as patent rights are viewed as questionable, patent litigators are incentivized to go after the rents that the patents protect. This is especially true if the patent is of significant commercial value and the patent holder is in a vulnerable position, having made a recent large capital investment, making it difficult for the owner to defend in court.

This has turned a patent into little more than a lottery ticket.[5] The filer of an accepted patent gets to reap the rewards of that patent until it expires or is sold. However, the expected payoff is contingent on it not being overturned in the courts and the potential cost of having to successfully defend the patent. On the other side of this argument, the filing of an invalid patent can serve as a roadblock to other innovators.

Indeed, many questionable patents exist, and sometimes, inventors complain about having to navigate a "patent thicket"[6] where a large number of idle patents sit waiting to block innovators or to command licensing fees. Once again, the holding of patents without actually using them to produce can be classified as rent seeking as firms use resources to find targets to execute their patent rights on without actually benefiting society whatsoever.

This is not to say that all uses of patents, or their licensing, are rent seeking. In fact, a healthy secondary market for patents and patent licensing serves as a means for fostering innovation, under the right conditions. Imagine for a moment that you are in possession of a patentable idea that you believe will be of significant commercial value someday. You decide to pursue this idea, hire a lawyer, file a patent, and even create a prototype. Assuming that the prototype works, at this point, the work of the inventor is essentially done.

What's needed now is, for lack of a better term, a businessperson. It's possible that you, the inventor, will want to see your invention through to the end like Bill Gates did with Microsoft and Steve Jobs did, in two stints, with Apple. Or perhaps, your interest is really just in the act of inventing, and although you'd like to get compensated for your innovation, you've no interest in actually going through the full process of making a viable business out of it.

In this situation, in the absence of a secondary market for patents, you would be forced to take your invention to market in order to make any money. If this process seems daunting to the inventor, they may never make their findings public, limiting the benefits of their innovation, or worse, they may not choose to invent at all. If they can license or sell the intellectual property rights to their invention, they get paid a portion of the resulting monopoly rents and free themselves up to embark on a new endeavor.

There is evidence that the creators of an invention are not always the best suited to actually run a business. For instance, Cisco's cofounders Len Bosack and Sandy Lerner found themselves ousted from Cisco Systems after the company began to grow faster than they could manage. They encountered tension between their desire to keep the company informal and the rigors required to grow their company. Relieved from their chief executive officer (CEO) duties, the entrepreneurs were continually at odds with their superiors. Sandy was eventually fired and Bosack, her husband, quit.[7] This suggests that, although the inventor plays an important role in the innovation process, having a robust secondary market for patents can improve social welfare by allowing inventors to sell their ideas to those who can make them commercially viable.

Although there are certainly benefits to secondary markets for patents, we need to be careful not to conflate having a market with the market being efficient. Yes, certainly there are efficiency gains from specialization; inventors should invent and business people should "business". But in the case of patent markets, we cannot lose sight of the fact that the market is fundamentally inefficient due to imperfect information. The patent filer surely knows more about the patent than those who approve it, purchase it, or license it do. This can lead to problems for purchasers of patent rights. Perhaps the seller knows that the patent is questionable or not commercially viable or both.

Regardless, this discussion of patents offers an interesting glimpse into an example of rent seeking. In this case, the government, by granting rights to monopoly rents, sows the seeds for fruitful rent seeking. However, it's the private marketplace, both through commercialization of patents and secondary markets for patents, that offers the incentives to rent seek. Furthermore, rent seeking takes place because patents are flawed in that they are imperfectly awarded. The legal battles, NPEs, and defensive aggregators all exist because existing patents can be overturned even after they have been awarded.

What to do? There are two possible outcomes. For one, the patent process could be made more rigorous and patents that are awarded could be guaranteed. This would eliminate legal challenges that result from having questionable patents. The other option is to abolish patents altogether. Both outcomes would eliminate the need for patent litigators, NPEs, and defensive aggregators to exist at all. Would we be sorry to see them go?

## Rubber hands and supercomputers

Thomas Peterffy is best known as the founder of Interactive Brokers, an online trading platform. With an estimated net worth of $18.8 billion, he is the richest person in Florida[8] and the 69th wealthiest person in the world.[9] However, Thomas Peterffy did not come from money. Instead, he came to the United States in 1965 as a refugee from then communist Hungary. Once in the United States, he developed a passion for programming and eventually for options markets and trading.

Back when Peterffy got his start trading in the 1970s and 1980s, the floors of the stock exchanges were chaotic places. Little technology was used, trades were executed with a phone call to a broker who would have to go and physically partake in an auction in order to execute a trade. The floors of the stock exchanges were full of gruff and boisterous traders trying to get their clients the best deals possible.

But Peterffy had a vision of bringing technology onto the trading floor and using computer programs to execute trades. So he equipped his floor traders with tablet computers capable of running his pricing algorithms to give his traders an edge. The tablets were met with resistance by other floor traders, especially after one caught fire. Finally, in 1987 with the advent of the NASDAQ's "Small Order Execution System", Peterffy was able to take his strategy to the confines of his offices and execute trades from behind a keyboard.[10]

However, Peterffy noticed that entering in trades was time-consuming. To reduce the latency of his trades, the time it takes for an order to be entered, processed, and executed, he decided to connect his own computer directly into the NASDAQ data feed, cutting out the need to use a keyboard. Noticing an abnormally large number of trades being executed by Peterffy's firm, regulators showed up to his office to find that he had spliced his computer directly into the NASDAQ data feed and that the computer was executing trades automatically. Unfortunately for Peterffy, this violated NASDAQ trading rules, which required that trades be executed using a keyboard. Undeterred, Peterffy and his engineers devised a typing robot with rubber fingers to automatically execute trades.[11]

With Thomas Peterffy's rubber hand, fully autonomous algorithmic trading was born. Following the NASDAQ, all other exchanges have implemented some form of electronic trading making the need for floor traders and brokers all but obsolete. So desolate has the trading floor become that cable news networks use the once-crowded and loud floor of the New York Stock Exchange as permanent cable television sets during the trading day.[12]

Needless to say, the implementation of trading technology has resulted in dramatic increases in market efficiency. Gone are the days where a small number of businesspeople got together and traded equity stakes in their companies face-to-face. Now sophisticated professional financial investors use real-time data, complex pricing models, and highly skilled workers to try to make money and beat the market.

To a certain extent, unsophisticated amateur financial investors have benefited from the implementation of technology as well. Almost all brokers offer some form of electronic trading for a nominal fee ($4.95 per trade) or even for free through popular trading apps accessible through your mobile phone. These reduced costs make investing in financial markets cheaper and more accessible than they have ever been.

However, changes in the structure of the financial markets have given rise to opportunities to rent seek. Like patent markets, financial markets are another interesting case study in that secondary financial markets are necessary in a well-functioning capitalist economy, but loosely regulated financial markets can lead to rent seeking. The excessive use of technology is one way that traders go about capturing rents.

Today's trading world is made up of a number of different types of financial investors. At the bottom of the totem pole is the private investor looking to speculate in the stock market. These unsophisticated financial investors tend to do little in-depth market research, do not have enough funds to properly diversify their portfolios, make a small number of trades, and hold their positions for a long period. Your run-of-the-mill institutional investors are more sophisticated than amateur investors, have teams that conduct market research, use sophisticated computer models to make forecasts, have very large portfolios, and make large numbers of very large trades. However, there are a select few financial investors who trade purely algorithmically and use supercomputers to execute their trades in fractions of a millisecond. These algorithmic traders have engineers, programmers, and PhDs write complex computer models to make forecasts and execute trades automatically. They have very large portfolios and rarely hold their positions for more than a second.

Now, all three of these market participants (the unsophisticated financial investor, the run-of-the-mill institutional investor, and the algorithmic investors) have the same goal in mind – to make money – but they all play the game a little bit differently. The private financial investor is hoping that their portfolio grows into a nice little nest egg so that they can retire. Institutional investors are looking to earn fees charged for executing trades, managing funds, selling financial assets, and so on. The algorithmic traders are looking to take advantage of anomalies in the market and make pennies per trade over a very large number of trades.

Of course, each market participant is looking to capture a rent. Consider the private investor, call him Joe Shmoe. When Joe Shmoe puts his money into the financial markets, he is taking some additional risk by not buying safer assets such as government bonds.[13] To minimize the risk of losing money, Joe does some research, selects a few companies that he thinks will be successful over the coming years and plunks down some of his hard-earned savings in the Wall Street casino. If Joe is lucky, most of his money goes into a stock like Apple. If he were lucky enough to buy in 1980, he would make a $56,000%-plus[14] return on his money. Surely, Joe would've been happy if his money increased tenfold over the same time period, meaning that Joe has earned a rent.

Likewise, institutional investors earn rents in the same way. But they have a number of other tools they can use to ensure that they make money. Some of them are on the up and up, some of them result from structural advantages, and some of them are purely the result of misinforming investors.

A large part of the returns generated by financial services firms come from superior skill. After all, large financial firms have huge sums of capital to put to work by investing in technology, data, and human capital. Simply by being professionals, those that spend their days working in finance are going to do a better job than the unsophisticated investor. That being said, we need not forget that the stock market is similar to a large state-sponsored casino. And let's be honest, if you were playing poker at a casino, who would you put your money on? You? Or the professional gambler sitting next to you?

But just because professional financial investors earn rents doesn't mean that they are rent seeking. In fact, much of what financial investors do is beneficial in a capitalist society. For one, primary financial markets provide funding for firms that need it. There are very few successful companies that do not require seed funding and the need for seed funding has increased from about half a million dollars in 2008 to roughly $2 million in 2018.[15] Subsequent rounds of funding allow rapidly growing companies to operate before becoming profitable. For technology companies especially, a lack of profitability often runs through their initial public offering. Only 17% of technology companies that had their initial public offering in 2017 were profitable down from 91% in 1980.[16]

To a certain extent, primary finance acts as a gatekeeper ensuring that commercially viable ideas move forward while less viable ideas never receive the funding needed to be brought to market. However, secondary financial markets are far less benign. The secondary market offers prolific opportunities to rent seek.

Secondary financial markets serve two main purposes: price discovery and providing the ability for financial investors to sell their stake in a company to take profits. In theory, both of these purposes improve economic efficiency. However, both of these functions also allow opportunities for abuse.

Within price discovery, there's significant debate as to how quickly that price discovery should occur. One avenue that traders can gain a structural advantage is through latency, or the amount of time it takes for a digital command to be executed. Low-latency trading is clearly not new. Compared to the open outcry trading of old, Peterffy's rubber hand machine was relatively low latency, and the algorithms he helped develop certainly aided in more accurate price discovery and liquidity.

Unfortunately, the continued drive for low latency has reached levels to which the social benefit of executing trades faster is virtually nonexistent. There is no reasonable argument in favor of trade latency levels measured in milliseconds. No rational financial investor would argue that being able to trade with that kind of speed actually improves market efficiency in any *socially* meaningful way. Instead, low-latency trading gives sophisticated investors with access to vast troves of capital and subscription data the ability to front-run price movements that would happen anyway, albeit at a slower pace. *Individual* market participants armed with the right tools stand to make fortunes.

As such, the competition over speed has become so fierce that firms have collocated, purchasing space for their servers, at the different exchanges and data centers. So sensitive are market participants to small changes in latency, data providers ensure a level playing field by precisely measuring the length of the fiber optic cables connecting their machines to the data feed. To highlight how absurd this is, the reason for such careful measurement is because the further the server is from the exchange, the longer it takes the command to execute because the *speed of light* is finite. Without connections of identical length, traders with identical technologies who were the closest to the data feed would get their orders in the fastest. Since latency trading is a winner take all competition, if you're not first, the trading opportunity you were trying to take advantage of is gone.[17]

The need for low latency has, arguably, gotten out of hand. In 2010, Spread Networks, now owned by Zayo, installed an 825-mile fiber optic cable between New York and Chicago in order to reduce trade latency by a mere 3 milliseconds over the next-fastest connection, a 925-mile cable.[18] The total cost of installing the cable was estimated to be $100 million per millisecond, money that would have had greater social use elsewhere.[19] Still, the pursuit of speed has not lessened. Even faster technologies like microwave and "millimeter wave networks" have been offered as competitors by NASDAQ.[20] The roundtrip latency of these networks is measured in microseconds, or thousandths of a millisecond. Although not available to transmit data over long distances like fiber optic networks, these systems make the transmission of data, for all practical purposes, instantaneous.

Being able to receive, process, and act on information faster than other market participants is akin to the fastest traders having "foreknowledge".[21] Although they cannot actually see into the future, by being able to process and act on information faster than other traders, relative to less sophisticated traders, they de facto can. With this foreknowledge in hand, sophisticated financial investors can profit from what amounts to an arbitrage opportunity.

In theory, having market participants take advantage of arbitrage opportunities improves market efficiency and social welfare. However, in the case of latency arbitrage (using superior trading speed to take advantage of incorrectly priced financial assets), the social benefit of such activities is suspect at best. Consider an example where a piece of news is released that will cause the value of a stock to change. As is required by law, all participants in the financial markets receive the information at the same time. However, due to the superior latency of some investors, it's as if they received the information microseconds before the rest of the market participants. In response, they either buy or sell the financial assets microseconds faster, capitalizing on the price movement that would happen regardless of their superior technology.

And although the technology is impressive, the purpose of the technology is to allow for trade orders to be processed more quickly. Remember, when it comes to trading on *secondary* financial markets, the direct result is simply a transfer of wealth from one party to another, and in this case, sophisticated investors are using a costly structural advantage in order to secure that wealth transfer. This use of resources for negligible increases in market efficiency is rent seeking.

To be clear, secondary financial markets play an important role in the health of the overall economy. Without them, it would be exceedingly difficult for companies to raise money. Primary financial investors would have an extremely difficult time trying to get their money out to apply it to a new venture. It would be far more difficult to assess the value of a company. The economy as a whole would be less transparent as privately owned companies do not have to make public their financial statements. In effect, secondary financial markets improve social welfare by fostering capital accumulation and growth,[22] ensuring that they are not purely rent seeking. As was outlined earlier, however, they provide ample opportunities to rent seek.

In chapter 12 of *The General Theory of Employment, Interest, and Money*, Keynes famously grapples with the role of secondary financial markets and their impact on investment[23] in physical capital. On one hand, Keynes agrees that secondary financial markets help increase the level of investment because it makes a businessperson's investment revocable. Secondary markets keep the entrepreneur from being tied to their investment decisions for life, freeing them up to make new investments, to enjoy their returns, or to abandon a failing firm.

On the other hand, Keynes argued that secondary financial markets can pose a threat to investment if they become too speculative. Once professional speculators take over, the social benefits of secondary financial markets are reduced. According to Keynes, speculators differ from financial investors in that speculators try to foresee "changes in the conventional basis of valuation a short time ahead of the general public"[24] while financial investors try to evaluate the long-term viability of companies. The former holds financial assets for short periods while the latter stays invested for the long term.

If markets are efficient, the existence of speculators does little harm to the financial system. Speculators trade assets at their fundamental value, hold them for a short time, and sell them at their fundamental value. Any profit made by the speculator is a result of a change in the underlying value of the asset. However, the requirements for efficient financial markets are not likely to exist in reality. Efficient financial markets require unrealistic assumptions like that all agents in the financial markets have "rational expectations". Under the rational expectations assumption, it is assumed that participants have all of the information relevant to the correct pricing of securities. The rational expectations assumption of the model assumes, in effect, that participants know all current and future cash flows of all securities traded on financial markets.[25]

Financial markets do not operate under the conditions necessary for them to be perfectly efficient. Sophisticated investors do their best to aggregate data and make educated decisions, but it is irrational to assume that anyone knows what will happen in the future or even the actual probability of future events. Instead, since the future is inherently unknowable, financial market participants fall back on rules of thumb and follow certain conventions when making price estimates, such as using market comparables rather than calculating value from the ground up. Worse still, less sophisticated investors,[26] who own about 20% of all equities in the United States,[27] do not have access to the time, skill, or resources needed to come up with correct valuations of financial assets.

Combined, the reliance on convention and the lack of sophistication of a large portion of investors give speculators plenty of trade fodder especially when the conventions underlying the price of financial assets change. These changes can be quite large and happen rapidly when asset prices are based on "the mass psychology of a large number of ignorant individuals".[28] As the number of unsophisticated investors grows, financial institutions find speculation to be more profitable than taking long positions, and the likelihood of having "correct" prices becomes impossible.

The result is that market volatility can be dramatically exacerbated during times of changing sentiment as sophisticated institutional investors try to profit off asset price swings. Knowing this, sophisticated investors have devoted a large portion of their time and resources trying to predict market sentiment as opposed to actually trying to estimate the long-term value and viability of companies. This has resulted in computers almost instantaneously executing trades based on current events and even tweets. It is akin to playing a high-speed high risk "game of Snap, of Old Maid, of Musical Chairs – a pastime in which he is victor . . . who passes the Old Maid to his neighbor before the game is over".[29]

The consequences of this are twofold. First, this type of speculative financial market is not socially optimal and results in a misallocation of resources as financial assets may be overpriced or underpriced solely due to market sentiment. This can cause capital to be allocated to projects that make sense as a short-run speculative gamble but may be less socially beneficial in the long run. Under these conditions, it becomes apparent that "[t]here is no clear evidence from experience that investment policy which is socially advantageous coincides with that which is most profitable".[30]

Second, the financial markets become vulnerable to misinformation and "flash crashes" as a larger portion of trades are taken out of the hands of humans and executed algorithmically. In both cases, stock prices and entire market indexes can decrease rapidly only to rebound back to their pre-crash value in a matter of minutes. These rapid movements can not only be incredibly profitable for algorithmic traders but can also undermine market confidence.

As an example, at 1:07 p.m. on April 23, 2013, the Associated Press released the following tweet: “Breaking: Two explosions in the White House and Barack Obama is injured”. At the time, the Dow Jones Industrial Average was up 134 points from its previous close. By 1:10 p.m. the Dow had fallen 147 (about 1%) below its 1:07-p.m. level. By 1:15 pm, after the tweet was discovered to be false, the market had recovered to the pre-tweet level. With cyberattacks and the dissemination of misinformation rising, as long as computers continue to comb social media for information, we are likely to see more events like this in the future. Although scary, and clearly based on inaccurate information, this “tweet crash” was relatively benign.

More severe “flash crashes” have resulted from what amounts to system errors as different trading algorithms get locked into some sort of reinforcing cycle. Perhaps the most famous is the flash crash of May 6, 2010. Between 2:32 p.m. and 2:46 p.m., the market found itself in near freefall, with the Dow falling to nearly 1,000 points (9.2%) below the previous day’s close. As was documented by the Securities and Exchange Commission,[31] the flash crash was triggered by a large automated sell order of S&P e-mini futures contracts. Initially, high-frequency trading firms absorbed the majority of the contracts sold; however, as external liquidity for the contracts began to dry up, high-frequency traders began to sell the contracts back and forth to one another, driving the price down even further and causing markets to plummet. At 2:45 p.m., trading in the e-mini futures market was paused for just five seconds and markets began recovering.

Short-term speculation in financial markets is rent seeking. Resources in the form of computers, programmers, data centers, fiber optic cables, and so on are allocated away from some other, more socially productive use. An argument could be made that under normal times, short-term trading satisfies the need for trades to be executed immediately. However, the underlying motive for high-frequency trading, speculative trading based on changes in market sentiment, has little to no social benefit. Instead, this type of activity can lead to negative social outcomes, like flash crashes and asset bubbles, as market positions are reversible for individuals while the resources they allocate are used up and no longer available for the rest of society.

## Bureaucracy, power, and influence

At one point in your career, you might find yourself sitting at your desk, staring at your computer screen, and thinking to yourself, “If I could just get them to listen to me, the company would be doing so much better!” Such is life for people who actually do the work, crunch the numbers, and implement management's plans but have no real decision-making power. Instead, the worker is essentially instructed by their bosses as to what they should do and they are evaluated based on whether they do their job as instructed. But what happens when workers really want to implement meaningful change? Oftentimes, it's rent seeking.

Surely this is a bit of a paradox, but workers without decision-making power trying to create change within an organization can end up wasting resources, most notably time, without actually being able to get their proposed changes implemented. Referred to as "influence costs",[32] this type of activity is akin to lobbying the government to implement changes in policy, except, in this case, the government isn't involved whatsoever.

This type of rent seeking happens most frequently at firms where decision-making power is highly centralized. Under this type of firm structure, workers have incentives to lobby for changes that benefit them directly even if the benefit to the company is small or even a net negative. If successful, this can lead to large changes in the distribution of resources within a firm based on the amount of time and energy devoted to influencing superiors.

In many instances, the changes implemented through intracompany lobbying are significant. Workers can influence management to adopt a new technology, mid-level management can lobby to redirect funding toward their departments, and executives can influence the board of directors to change executive compensation policies. As a result of the lobbying, no output gets produced, the distribution of resources within the firm has changed, and resources, most notably time, have been wasted. Worse still, if the lobbying is not successful, the resources are wasted, full stop.

This is not to say that firms don't want their workers to spend time trying to enact meaningful change. Surely, who better to propose solutions to complicated problems than the workers who actually do the work. The problem is that workers, like their bosses, are self-interested. They need the company to do well, but wouldn't it be great if the company did well and a process that they were an expert in got implemented? That would make them more valuable to the firm with a greater potential to increase their income even if the suggestion is not the best option available for the firm.

Even though workers lobby for changes, it's the people with real decision-making power who have the greatest incentive to rent seek. In the worst cases, executive-level rent seeking amounts to nothing less than fraud, but in others, the executive behavior is seemingly benign. Regardless, rents tend to accrue to workers at high levels in companies because they have decision-making power and, perhaps more important, their contribution to the firm is more difficult to observe and measure.

Consider a worker whose job it is to fillet fish. On any given day, the worker is delivered more fish than they could possibly fillet, meaning that the productivity of the worker is not subject to a shortage of work. At the end of the day, the manager could go down to the worker's station, count the number of fillets, check the quality of their work, and directly observe what the worker's contribution to the firm was that day. Based on those observations, the company could pay that worker exactly the value that they added.

When thinking about the contribution of executives, the problem becomes much more complicated. On any given day, an executive may monitor workers, hold meetings, respond to emails, make phone calls, raise money, strategize, and so forth. However, measuring the contribution of these activities is notoriously difficult, in part because it is not clear that anyone actually monitors what they do on any given day. Additionally, even if a CEO's day was perfectly observable, it's not clear that their contribution could be accurately measured, not even by the overall performance of the company. As such, the payment going to executives is largely determined outside of their marginal product because it's not clear what their marginal product is.

So how is executive pay determined? It's not entirely clear. During the shareholder value movement, there has been a tendency toward "performance-based" pay. This means that executives receive a larger portion of their compensation in the form of stock options and less in terms of salaries and bonuses. In the 1930s, the share of CEO pay at the largest 50 companies in the form of salary and bonuses was 100%. In 2014, salary and bonus compensation composed only 36% of total compensation while stock and options compensation accounted for 60% of CEO pay.[33]

At first glance, this seems like a good way to structure executive pay given that their day to day contribution is mostly unobservable. It makes sense that a CEO's income should be tied to how well their company does as their primary role is to manage the company and set a strategy for the firm. However, the structure of this compensation matters quite a bit as CEOs can be compensated handsomely simply for working in a growing sector even though the company they manage is a laggard. Even worse, once a compensation contract is set, the CEO can extract rents by strategizing to reach certain markers even if those strategies end up being bad for the longer-term health of the firm.

Under the corporate governance structure for large corporations, CEOs do not have the power to set their own pay structures. The reasons for this are somewhat obvious; if a CEO had the ability to set their own compensation, they would simply set it to be as high as possible without breaching some sort of mutiny constraint. Instead, CEOs rely on a company's board of directors to set their compensation. However, pay negotiations are usually not arm's-length negotiations, as CEOs tend to serve on the board of directors not only of their own firm but on other firms as well. This allows CEOs to indirectly set the market for their own compensation, along with other corporate governance decisions, and these decisions propagate across firms.[34]

And changes in CEO compensation structures vary, in part, due to changes external to the firm. For instance, the coming of age of the shareholder value movement played a role in shifting CEO pay compensation away from salaries and towards performance compensation. In and of itself, this is not a strange transition. However, coupled with the tax reform in the 1950s that allowed options to be taxed at a lower capital gains rate, it becomes clear that some changes in compensation structure are designed to maximize CEO disposable income.

On the surface, this is not nefarious. Economic agents should act in their own best interest. CEOs and the boards of directors don't want to leave money on the table. However, over time, tax reform can have significant impacts on the behavior of executives as it can incentivize rent seeking as the rewards for rent seeking are increased. This is especially true if the income received is taxed at a flat rate that's lower than the tax rate on ordinary income.

In addition to influencing their own compensation, executives with decision-making power over company processes and systems can increase their importance to the firm by adopting specialized software, accounting practices, organizational structures, hiring from their existing network, and so forth. If these processes are complex enough, it may be too costly to replace the company expert, making them invaluable to the firm. Alternatively, executives who want to find alternative employment may use company resources to make themselves more visible and attractive to other firms. This could include going to an industry conference on the company's dime and inquiring about the availability of jobs at other attendees' companies. Or employees may use company resources to obtain training and credentials that they then take elsewhere.[35]

Another way that managers can rent seek is through their appetite for risk. For instance, a savvy manager may suggest the company undertake a risky strategy knowing that if they are right, the payoff would be substantial. However, if they are wrong and the project's failure is not yet observable by outside firms, they can abandon the project and the company before being associated with the failure.[36] Similarly, managers may choose projects that are closely aligned to their personal skills even if they are not profit-maximizing for the firm.[37] This may make the manager appear to excel at their job. In reality, they are choosing a strategy that is good for them but suboptimal for the firm as a whole.

In all, managers by design wield a significant amount of power and influence within the modern corporate structure. Unfortunately, because the activities of managers are largely unobservable it is hard to quantify exactly what their marginal product for the firm is. This is problematic when it comes to setting compensation. Under societal structures that place a large amount of emphasis on money as a measure of prestige, and where the penalty to making more money is small, individuals have a greater incentive to try to extract money from firms; they have an incentive to rent seek.

## It's not just the rich

Although powerful individuals have a lot to gain from rent seeking, it must be noted that rent seeking takes place across income brackets. Unionized workers, for instance, earn significantly more than their nonunionized peers. Workers are hired in droves to leave reviews for products at online retailers' websites such as Amazon. Even when power is decentralized (in a cooperative, for example), workers spend time lobbying their peers to gain support for their initiative. Faculty members are notorious for organizing to ensure that they present a unified view to the administration and board of directors.

Unskilled workers, when they rent seek, do so in ways that are significantly different than when executives rent seek. For instance, prior to GPS technology, truck drivers could not be tracked in real time by their managers. They could, within limits, move at their own speed. Of course, the trucking company would have an idea of how long it should take to drive a certain route, but traffic is notoriously unpredictable. What's to stop a trucker from taking an extended break if they are making good time and blame a small delay on traffic?[38] In fact, any scenario in which the monitoring of workers is imperfect, workers have an incentive to shirk and "steal time" from their employers by being off the job but on the clock. Through the efficiency wage lens, firms are forced to pay workers rents in order to make the consequences of losing their job high enough to prevent them from slacking off.

Much like the unobservable executive, workers may receive higher wages when their contribution to the firm is hard to quantify. However, there is one key difference, firms can easily hold workers accountable, workers cannot hold executives and boards of directors accountable. Truckers, for instance, have fallen victim to increased monitoring technologies through the advent and implementation of GPS and traffic tracking. Long gone are the days of detours and stops that could be explained away by some unseen delay as increased monitoring has all but eliminated the need to pay an above-market wage to extract effort. Through increased monitoring, firms have shifted rents away from workers and toward executives through improved efficiency.

And here is where the link between the concentration of income and rents becomes clear. Rents are everywhere, no market is perfectly competitive, but when power lies in the hands of the very few, it's easy for them to lay claim to rents. Implementing a new process that improves efficiency across a firm becomes the property of those in charge even if it's achieved on the backs of their workers. Worse still, sometimes those "efficiency gains" aren't really gains at all, they're just a shifting of rents and society is no better off because of them. It's simply a power grab.

## The complacent economists

Of course, economists themselves need to carry at least some of the blame for the existence of rent seeking. Within standard economic theory, there is an undertone of fairness. The thought process goes something like this, workers get paid their marginal products, capital receives its marginal product, and perfectly competitive markets are efficient. Under such a market system, social welfare is maximized through competition. As a result, rent seeking does not exist because there are no rents to seek.

But economists, and the average human being, know that the reality we experience is drastically different. Market power is concentrated among firms. Workers produce more than they are paid for, resulting in profits. And economic agents spend time, energy, and resources trying to claim an ever-growing piece of the pie for themselves. And who should blame them? After all, the archetypical economic agent is a cold, calculating self-interested machine that looks only to maximize their utility. Like it or not, economics has led to an increase in such behavior and individualism.

And yet, for years, economists fascinated themselves with building models that mathematically demonstrated the ideal economy, whereby economic profits were eliminated and social welfare was maximized. While all this was going on, seemingly nobody who was deemed to be a serious person in economics stopped to contemplate whether any capitalist economy actually demonstrated the properties that they were so fascinated with.

Out of this paradigm came justification for everyone's income. The mystical market determined everyone's wage by somehow determining what their marginal product was. Their income was *justified.* So long as no central body interfered and markets were allowed to operate how God intended, there was no room for complaint. The economic system was fair, power was unimportant, and any discrepancies, such as discrimination, would be solved by market mechanisms dubbed "the invisible hand".

There is, of course, a problem with such a fantasy. Power and influence do exist, and as well-trained economic agents, powerful people will wield it for their own benefit. Much like the free-market boogeyman, the government, these agents will distort the market. If they're good at what they do, their power and influence will become even more concentrated and the economists' model even more distorted. When the system distorts, rents appear and the powerful, acting exactly how they should, go out and claim them for themselves.

This is the paradox of capitalism. A system set up to be fair, set up to maximize social welfare, and set up to reward people for their hard work fails to deliver fairness. Those who benefit from the system proclaim that the system is indeed fair, what they've *earned* is the result of their hard work and the rewards they received aren't determined by them but rather some external "market forces". Those who find themselves powerless and vulnerable to the whims of the economy feel cheated and cry foul. They work more than one job, well over 40 hours a week, and still feel like they can't get ahead.

As a result, they resent the winners. But their ability to muster a response is limited. After all, they live in a system that proclaims it's a meritocracy and that differences in success are explained away by differences in skills, abilities, work ethic, and foresight. They look up to the winners and aspire to be like them. Or if not for the good of themselves, they posture for their children to be like them. They all seek the rents.

## Notes


1 Theranos (n.d.). Crunchbase. Retrieved from www.crunchbase.com/organization/theranos
2 Carreyrou, John (2018). *Bad blood: Secrets and lies in a Silicon Valley startup* (First ed.). New York: Knopf.
3 Patent FAQs (n.d.). [Text]. Retrieved from www.uspto.gov/help/patent-help
4 Hagiu, Andrei, & Yoffie, David B. (2013). The New Patent Intermediaries: Platforms, Defensive Aggregators, and Super-Aggregators. *Journal of Economic Perspectives*, *27*(1), 45–66. https://doi.org/10.1257/jep.27.1.45
5 Lemley, Mark A., & Shapiro, Carl (2005). Probabilistic Patents. *Journal of Economic Perspectives*, *19*(2), 75–98. https://doi.org/10.1257/0895330054048650
6 Shapiro, Carl (2001). Navigating the Patent Thicket: Cross Licenses, Patent Pools, and Standard Setting. In A. Jaffe, J. Lerner, & S. Stern, eds., *Innovation Policy and the Economy*, volume 1. MIT Press. Cambridge, Massachusetts.
7 Davila, Antonio, Foster, George, & Jia, Ning (2010). Building Sustainable High-Growth Startup Companies: Management Systems as an Accelerator. *California Management Review*, *52*(3), 79. https://doi.org/10.1525/cmr.2010.52.3.79
8 Wang, Jennifer, & Kirsch, Noah (n.d.). The Richest Person in Each State 2019. Retrieved from www.forbes.com/sites/jenniferwang/2019/06/26/the-richest-person-in-each-state-2019/#2b7c78e280d8
9 Bloomberg Billionaires Index (n.d.). Retrieved from www.bloomberg.com/billionaires/
10 Simpson, Stephen D. (2019, June 25). The Death of the Trading Floor. *Investopedia*. Retrieved from www.investopedia.com/financial-edge/0511/the-death-of-the-trading-floor.aspx

11 Kestenbaum, David (2015, April 23). "We Built a Robot That Types": The Man Behind Computerized Stock Trading. *NPR.Org*. Retrieved from www.npr.org/2015/04/23/401781306/we-built-a-robot-that-types-the-man-behind-computerized-stock-trading
12 Levine, D. M. (2013, May 29). A Day in the Quiet Life of a NYSE Floor Trader. *Fortune*. https://fortune.com/2013/05/29/a-day-in-the-quiet-life-of-a-nyse-floor-trader/
13 Some governments are obviously riskier than others. However, government bonds are often thought of as "risk-free".
14 Investopedia (2019, September 20). If You Had Invested Right After Apple's IPO. *Investopedia*. Retrieved from www.investopedia.com/articles/active-trading/080715/if-you-would-have-invested-right-after-apples-ipo.asp
15 PitchBook (2019, January 28). 18 Charts to Illustrate US VC in 2018. Retrieved from https://pitchbook.com/news/articles/18-charts-to-illustrate-us-vc-in-2018
16 Ritter, Jay R. (2020, March 18). Initial Public Offerings: Updated Statistics. Retrieved from https://site.warrington.ufl.edu/ritter/files/IPOs2019Statistics_Mar18_2020.pdf
17 Baron, Matthew, Brogaard, Jonathan, Hagströmer, Björn, & Kirilenko, Andrei (2019). Risk and Return in High-Frequency Trading. *Journal of Financial and Quantitative Analysis*, *54*(3), 993–1024.
18 Steiner, C. (2010, September 9). Wall Street's Speed War. *Forbes*. Retrieved from www.forbes.com/forbes/2010/0927/outfront-netscape-jim-barksdale-daniel-spivey-wall-street-speed-war.html
19 Budish, Eric, Cramton, Peter, & Shim, John (2015). The High-Frequency Trading Arms Race: Frequent Batch Auctions as a Market Design Response. *The Quarterly Journal of Economics*, *130*(4), 1547–1621.
20 *NASDAQ Co-Location* (n.d.). Retrieved from http://nasdaqtrader.com/Trader.aspx?id=colo
21 Hirshleifer, Jack (1971). The Private and Social Value of Information and the Reward to Inventive Activity. *American Economic Review*, *61*(4), 561–574; Fama, Eugene F., & Laffer, Arthur B. (1971). Information and Capital Markets. *Journal of Business*, *44*(3), 289–298.
22 For instance, see Lopez, Jose A., & Spiegel, Mark M. (2002). Financial Structure and Macroeconomic Performance Over the Short and Long Run. *Pacific Basin Working Paper Series* 2002–05, Federal Reserve Bank of San Francisco.
23 Here investment needs to be distinguished from financial investment. Investment is the purchase of new capital equipment or business inventories whereas financial investment is the purchase of a financial or paper asset.
24 Keynes, J. M. (1936). *The General Theory of Employment, Interest, and Money* (First edition). New York: Harcourt, Brace & World, p. 154.
25 See Crotty, James (2011). The Realism of Assumptions Does Matter: Why Keynes-Minsky Theory Must Replace Efficient Market Theory as the Guide to Financial Regulation Policy. *Economics Department Working Paper Series. 113*. Retrieved from https://scholarworks.umass.edu/econ_workingpaper/113 for an extensive discussion of the absurdity of the assumptions underlying the CAPM model and efficient market hypothesis. Crotty (2011).
26 Noninstitutional.
27 McGrath, Charles (2017, April 25). *80% of Equity Market Cap Held by Institutions*. Pensions & Investments. Retrieved from www.pionline.com/article/20170425/INTERACTIVE/170429926/80-of-equity-market-cap-held-by-institutions

28 Keynes (1936).
29 Keynes (1936), pp. 155–156.
30 Keynes (1936), p. 157.
31 Findings Regarding the Market Events of May 6, 2010: Report of the Staffs of the CFTC and SEC to the Joint Advisory Committee on Emerging Regulatory Issues (2010). Retrieved from www.sec.gov/news/studies/2010/marketevents-report.pdf
32 Milgrom, Paul R. (1988). Employment Contracts, Influence Activities, and Efficient Organization Design. *Journal of Political Economy*, *96*(1), 42–60. Retrieved from www.jstor.org/action/showPublication?journalCode=jpoliecon
33 Edmans, A., & Gabaix, X. (2017, June 26). Executive Compensation: A Survey of Theory and Evidence. Retrieved from https://scholar.harvard.edu/files/xgabaix/files/executive_compensation.pdf
34 Bouwman, Christina H. S. (2011). Corporate Governance Propagation Through Overlapping Directors. *Review of Financial Studies*, *24*(7), 2358–2394. https://doi.org/10.1093/rfs/hhr034
35 Scharfstein, David S., & Stein, Jeremy C. (2000). The Dark Side of Internal Capital Markets: Divisional Rent Seeking and Inefficient Investment. *The Journal of Finance*, *55*(6), 2537–2564.
36 Edlin, Aaron S., & Stiglitz, Joe E. (1995). Discouraging Rivals: Managerial Rent Seeking and Economic Inefficiencies. *The American Economic Review*, *85*(5), 1301–1312.
37 Shleifer, Andrei, & Vishny, Robert W. (1989). Management Entrenchment: The Case of Manager-Specific Investments. *Journal of Financial Economics*, *25*(1), 123–139.
38 Skott, Peter, & Guy, Frederick (2007). A Model of Power-biased Technological Change. *Economics Letters*, *95*(1), 124–131.

# 4 Education and the allocation of talent

The previous chapter outlined some examples of rent seeking, argued that rents tend to concentrate in the hands of the very few, and suggested that the capitalist system, built on the ideal of fairness, picked winners and losers based on merit. This final point has led many researchers to focus their attention on how to level the playing field. Since the economy is supposed to reward skill, what better way to level the playing field than through education?

As a result, there have been countless papers, studies, and books that look to explain differences in not only an individual's income but a country's gross domestic product (GDP) through the lens of education. Success, as defined by income and GDP, is considered obtainable through education. As a result, much time has been spent carefully defining human capital,[1] explaining how differences in human capital lead to differences between countries' growth rates[2] and how increased income inequality is, at least in part, the result of technological change that benefits those with a certain skill set.[3]

Certainly, educational attainment plays an important role in determining the overall well-being of a society. A majority of economists would likely agree that increasing the educational attainment of a country, even an already highly educated country like the United States, would reap benefits for the country as a whole. After all, there's overwhelming evidence that higher levels of education are linked to higher GDP, increased life expectancy, reduced poverty, better climate outcomes, and a more civically engaged population.

The democratization of higher education, the idea that it should be accessible to everyone, led the government to contribute to the funding of higher education. This was equally an economic stance as well as a moral one. Policies like the Morill Land-Grant Acts, which used the sale of public land to established public universities in areas that previously had none; Pell Grants; and government-sponsored loans placed increased pressure on universities, especially public universities, to provide evidence that there was a positive return on taxpayer dollars.

Famous papers, such as “A Contribution to the Empirics of Economic Growth” (1992),[4] received a lot of attention for showing that increasing educational attainment does indeed increase the growth rate of an economy. As a result, policymakers in developed and developing countries alike throw money at education in the hope of increasing the productive capacity of their countries. And to be sure, countries are better off due to their more educated workforce.

Furthermore, individuals reap significant gains from obtaining an education. In terms of income alone, in 2018 people with a high school degree had a median income of $730 per week compared to just $553 for their non-high-school-diploma-holding counterparts. Continuing on to obtain a bachelor’s degree ups median earnings to $1,198 per week, and obtaining a professional degree results in median earnings $1,884 – just over 3.4 times the median weekly earnings of Americans without a high school diploma![5]

In addition, educated workers find themselves far more likely to be employed. In 2018, workers without a high school diploma had an unemployment rate of 5.6% while those with professional degrees had an unemployment rate of 1.5%. With such significant economic benefits of education for the individual, households across the United States have enormous financial investments into their own, or their children’s, future.

Not surprisingly, due to the returns to education, particularly postsecondary education, American households have more than tripled their student loan debt outstanding from roughly $481 billion in 2006 to just over $1.6 trillion in 2019.[6] Is it worth it? For most, the answer is probably yes. All in, the average cost of one year of schooling, including tuition, fees, and room and board, at four-year institutions in the United States was $26,593. This is just a little more than the difference in median earnings between people who work full-time with a bachelor’s degree and those who just have a high school diploma, $24,336, meaning that by year 5, obtaining a bachelor’s degree has already paid for itself, on average.

Given that education has exhaustibly shown to benefit individuals and society as a whole, it seems futile to suggest that there might be a dark side to the pursuit of higher levels of educational attainment. But just because increasing the average educational attainment is good for an individual and good for a country doesn’t mean that its returns are optimized. What happens if we imagine that education is also intimately linked to rent seeking? Would our views on education policy change? I think so.

## Opportunities squandered?

Exceptional talent in any field, activity, or discipline is hard to come by. When an exceptionally talented individual is found, they tend to drive that field forward. In medicine, they could cure cancer, quickly develop a vaccine for a novel disease, or reduce mortality by perfecting organ transplants. And surely, society would be better off if exceptionally talented people went into fields with high social benefits. But there's a problem, as noted by Sendhil Mullainathan:

> Many of the best students are not going to research cancer, teach and inspire the next generation, or embark on careers in public service. Instead, large numbers are becoming traders, brokers and bankers. At Harvard in 2014, nearly one in five students who took a job went to finance. For economics majors, the number was closer to one in two. I can't help wondering: Is this the best use of talent?[7]

In our modern capitalist economy, people don't tend to measure their self-worth based on their contribution to society. Sure, it matters to people. Ask anyone who works in finance, consulting, or as a lawyer about their contributions to society and they'll either admit a weak social mission or mumble an answer about how everyone is better off because of what they do. But usually, people who work in rent-seeking-related fields do what they do because they're rightfully self-interested.[8] On top of that, in a consumerist society, people tend to measure themselves against their peers based on what they can afford, not by what they contribute. This social norm leads extremely talented young people to specialize in skills that maximize their personal income and not their potential benefit to society.

It's not hard to imagine that once people start thinking about education as being closely tied to income, its recipients become increasingly more interested in the return on their investment. However, the emphasis on post-secondary education being a springboard to prosperity is something that is relatively new. In their infancy, colleges were founded in the United States primarily as religious institutions whose goal was to train the next generation of clergy. The Founding Fathers even debated the merits of a national "institution" to homogenize the citizenry and teach the science of government.[9] Enrollment in these institutions was primarily restricted to the very-well-off, and employment was not the end goal.

This commoditization, or capitalization, of education helped give rise to the idea that education should have a monetary return. As such, it's no surprise that students pursue degrees that they think will reap the largest rewards and that promise them the largest rents. Coupling this with the behavior of businesses and their human resources departments, universities have gone from educating the clergy to being responsible for minting the next generation of human capital to be inserted directly into businesses' production functions. For some economists, myself included, discrete levels of education serve as signals to prospective employers and distinguish "high-skill" workers, who *can* perform a distinct set of tasks, from "low-skill" workers, who *will* perform a different set of tasks.[10]

Once we take this approach to human beings, that they are inputs into a production function, it's not hard to make the leap that their education should be thought of as a form of investment.[11] From the Keynesian perspective, any investments made are irreversible. Once resources are used, society cannot get those resources back.[12] So when society spends resources to educate its workforce, it seems to only make sense to think carefully about what skills its workforce is acquiring.

At the elementary school level, decisions about education are fairly uniform. Students are taught basic verbal and math literacy and are exposed to the arts, physical education, science, and so forth. Educators do this not because students are interested in all these topics[13] but because society finds it beneficial to teach students these elementary skills. However, once students are allowed to choose their field of study at the postsecondary level, society's job is mostly done, and students are allowed to choose to acquire skills in essentially whatever area they want.

How do people choose to acquire skills? At a very young age, toddlers tend to mimic things that their parents, siblings, and caregivers do. As they age, not much changes. Students observe what is going on around them; consider the advice of their peers, teachers, and mentors; and decide to specialize in fields that harmonize their interests and financial prospects. In doing so, they have made an individual investment. However, this investment may or may not be what a benevolent social planner[14] would have chosen. We should be far more concerned about students' choice of field of study than we are today. This is especially true as students continually decide to go to college with career aspirations in mind.[15]

Recall that in Chapter 2 we developed a working definition of rent seeking and offered up a few examples. People like lawyers, financiers, and executives all partook in rent-seeking activities as a result of imperfect regulation, innovation, intra-firm lobbying, and decision-making power. Across all these rent seeking roles lies a common denominator: they all generally require a college degree. Economists don't think carefully enough about the relationship between individual labor-market outcomes for graduates and the social consequences of those choices. To put it more bluntly, once society's elites have incomes that are made up mostly of rents, what is the social consequence of graduating students who aspire to follow in their footsteps?

In 1991, economists Kevin Murphy, Andrei Shleifer, and Robert Vishny made a seemingly obvious but important observation. When the most talented people in a country are put to good use, when they start firms and innovate, that country grows faster. However, if the most talented individuals are squandered by working in rent seeking occupations that country grows more slowly. Like most things in economics, this statement is logical and commonly accepted as being true, but to meet the criterion of economic truth, a much harder task must be undertaken, showing it in the data.

Unfortunately, it's hard, if not impossible, to directly measure the level of private rent seeking. Some authors have used corruption convictions by state to approximate the level of rent seeking.[16] Others use the number of lawyers in a given country[17] or the amount of government consumption and the number of coups.[18] Although innovative, all these authors are excluding a wide array of rent seeking behaviors from their analysis and do not capture the allocation of the most talented individuals, who presumably choose to go to college. To deal with the inability to observe rent seeking directly and to preserve their focus on the allocation of talent, Murphy, Shleifer, and Vishny use what students decide to study in college as an indicator of rent seeking.[19] They find that countries that educate a larger proportion of lawyers, rent seekers, grow more slowly than those who educate a higher proportion of STEM (science, technology, engineering, and mathematics) students, innovators.

However, rent seekers take many different forms than just lawyers. In the case of patent litigators, they are certainly lawyers. However, once we open up the possibility that rent seekers exist in the financial markets and within firms themselves, using just lawyers as a proxy for the level of rent seeking is far too conservative. This is especially true once we consider that, broadly speaking, the wealthiest individuals continue to receive an increasing proportion of their income in the form of rents. Instead, a holistic measure of rent seekers should include a broader range of businesspeople. Ultimately, economics students are far more likely to find themselves in a rent seeking role than a computer programmer.[20]

One possible way of testing this broader classification of rent seeking would be to try to replicate the Murphy et al. study with a broader list of majors classified as rent seeking. However, studies that use a large number of countries have significant shortcomings. To start, countries are culturally very different. This makes an apple to apple comparison difficult if not unconvincing. Additionally, the skills and knowledge needed to complete a four-year bachelor's degree in the United States are very different from a three-year bachelor's degree in the United Kingdom; forget Ethiopia. With large differences in educational attainment by country, an additional business major might contribute to the prospect of economic growth differently in a highly developed country than in a developing country. Add to that the difficulties in obtaining data and you have a recipe for disaster.

So where to look? We could try to find a place with a fairly homogenous culture, a large number of territories, degrees that are similar in their graduation requirements, comparable data over a large number of years . . . why not the United States?

## Future innovators and rent seekers: the composition of US undergraduates

Given its obsession with education, it should come as no surprise that the United States has a vast collection of education data. When it comes to obtaining data for universities in the United States, the Integrated Post-secondary Education Data System (IPEDS) has a trove of information on things like enrollment, institutions' finances, student financial aid, and degree completions at the individual school level.

What makes the IPEDS data particularly useful for thinking about rent seeking and the allocation of talent is that it tracks degree completions for all Title IV[21] institutions at the individual major level. In the system, there are nearly 1,000 unique majors at approximately 7,000 postsecondary institutions ranging from "floriculture/floristry operations management" to "laser and optical engineering" to "viticulture and enology".

Recall that the working hypothesis of Murphy et al. is that *countries* that graduate a higher proportion of lawyers grow more slowly than *countries* that graduate a higher proportion of engineers. To find out if this is true in the United States, we have to think carefully about the possible relationship between the composition of degree completions at the state level and growth. Before moving on to the analysis, it is important to establish three things: first, that there is at least some evidence that students respond to economic conditions at the state level; second, that there is sufficient variation in degree completions to develop a meaningful relationship between the composition of degree completions and growth; and, finally, a method to divide up majors by type, rent-related versus STEM-related.

When thinking about state-level conditions, using the composition of degrees for all new graduates in a state may not be the best indicator. Because there are no restrictions on migration within the United States, students are free to get a degree in one state and employment in another. One simple solution would be to find data on the number of existing graduates by major field of study within a state. Unfortunately, those data do not exist. So, until new data become available, the next best option is to use the composition of new degree completions within a state to approximate perceived career opportunities for talented individuals within that state.

That being said, migration is a problem that has to be considered. Migration is primarily a problem for a state like Massachusetts with globally prestigious schools like Harvard, MIT, Williams, and Amherst College. A large number of students from all over the country and all over the world choose to attend school in Massachusetts and leave after they graduate. From 1990 to 2018, public bachelor's degrees never exceed 34% of the total degree completions in the state. However, students who attend private colleges in

Massachusetts are far more likely to gain employment outside of the state. In total, four years after graduating only about 38% of graduates of private colleges in Massachusetts are employed within the state. The rest go off and seek employment elsewhere. On the other hand, graduates of public post-secondary institutions are far more likely to stay within the state after graduation. In Massachusetts, 60% of public college graduates were employed within the state four years after graduation.[22]

So, although it is reasonable to look at the percentage of all graduates in a state as representative of the structure of a state's economy, to mitigate concerns about migration it makes the most sense to look at only public postsecondary graduates. The appeal of this is twofold. First, graduates of public colleges and universities are far more likely to seek employment within the state and will therefore be more likely to gain skills that prepare them for local employment. Second, public universities are, at least in part, state-funded.[23] Policymakers are no doubt interested in knowing what their constituents' taxpayer dollars are funding.

## Funding the future: composition of degrees at public institutions

Figure 4.1[24] shows the number of mathematics, computer science, business, and legal studies degree completions at public postsecondary institutions in the United States. In addition to the sheer number of business degrees awarded, it appears that students' choice of major responds to economic

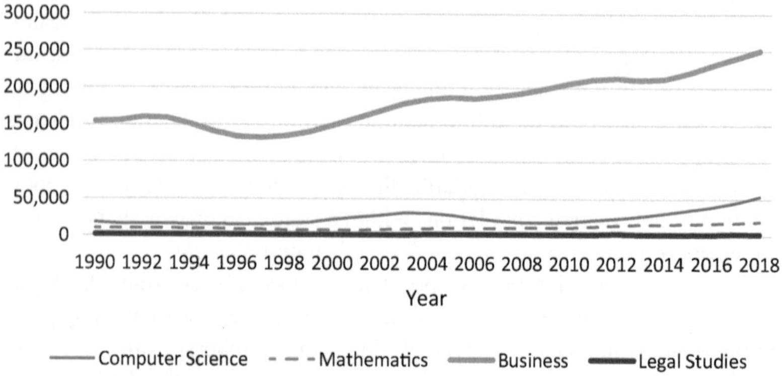


*Figure 4.1* Public school bachelor's degree completions for selected majors for the United States, 1990–2018

Source: Author's calculations using IPEDS.

conditions. For instance, degrees in computer science began to increase significantly in 1997 right around the onset of the dot-com bubble. What's even more remarkable is that computer science degree completions peaked in May 2003, lagging three years behind the record highs of NASDAQ set in February 2000. Following the burst of the dot-com bubble, the NASDAQ failed to set a new record high until November 2014, and it wasn't until the late aughts that computer science major degree completions began to recover. It took until the 2015 academic year for computer science degree completions to reach their 2003 peak levels, and they have risen ever since as technology-related industries continue to grow.

Similar economic events are visible in the number of business degree completions. Because we cannot infer anything pre-1990, it is hard to say exactly what kind of impact the savings-and-loans crisis of the 1980s and 1990s had on the number of business degree completions. However, the decrease in business degree completions between 1993 and 1997 (Figure 4.1) may be partially attributable to the savings and loan crisis that ended in 1995. There is a smaller drop in business degree completions following the dot-com bubble bust in 2000 and the financial crisis of 2007–2009. Once again, the number of business degree completions peaks 2012, exactly four class years after the S&P 500 peak in October 2007. The S&P 500 hit its cyclical low in February 2009, and business degree completions hit their cyclical low in 2013 before rebounding through the remainder of the time series.

Although we cannot say for certain whether student views around economic events truly cause movements in the composition of US degree completions, the timing of the peaks and troughs in degree completions by major suggests that students respond to postgraduation employment opportunities. When better opportunities exist in a particular major, students run off and get degrees in things like computer science and business.

When looking at the state-level data, the major trends in public degree completions through the dot-com bubble and the financial crisis are visible in most states. However, some more durable trends in public degree completions are visibly different. In levels, it is easiest to see the differences in these trends in the states that graduate a large number of students like California, New York, Florida, Texas, Pennsylvania, Massachusetts, and Michigan.

What's clear from looking at degree completions for each state is that the number of degrees awarded by major varies by state. In all states, the number of business degree completions far exceed those in computer science, mathematics, and legal studies (Figure 4.2). However, the trend of these degree completions varies dramatically. California, Florida, New York, and Texas see robust growth in the number of business degree completions while Michigan and Massachusetts do not.

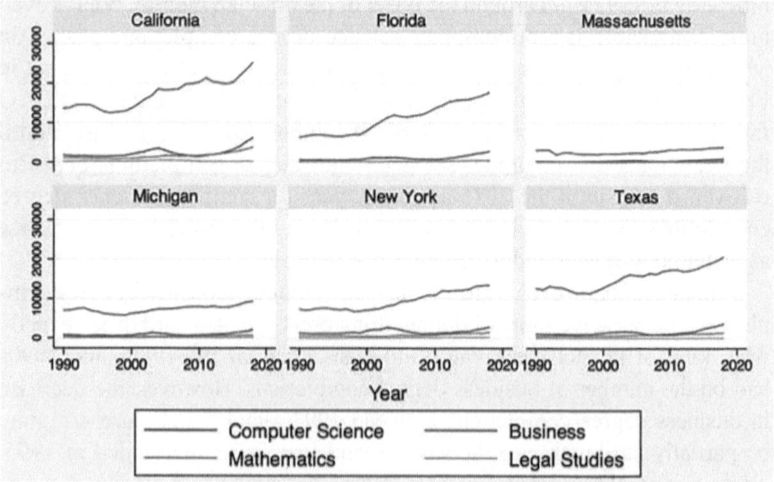


*Figure 4.2* Selected public school degree completions by selected states and majors, 1990–2018

Source: Author's calculations using IPEDS.

What's somewhat surprising is that not all states experienced the dot-com bubble in the same way. In California and New York, the dot-com bubble is very pronounced, with a steep rise in the number of computer science majors followed by a substantial collapse. The rapid increase in the number of computer science majors implies that the number of degree completions in any given field is not supply-constrained. Colleges and universities appear to stand ready to increase the number of available seats for a given major in response to a large increase in demand for that major. Florida only experiences a modest uptick in the number of computer science degree completions, but the downturn is far smaller than in California and New York.

The obvious question to ask is, Why? Why does the composition of degree completions by state vary so widely? These questions are extremely difficult to answer and the supply of college seats may play a role. It's entirely possible that during the mid-1990s, Texas computer science degrees were hard to come by just because Texas-based public universities were unable to find qualified people to teach the courses. Or perhaps Texas was unwilling to invest in new computers and computer labs meaning that even if they wanted to hire more computer science professors, Texas would be unable to give them a classroom to teach in. But why then were California and

New York able to increase the number of computer science students so dramatically?

However, the argument is weakened by the fact that, more recently, Texas was able to increase the number of computer science degree completions to levels significantly above their dot-com bubble peak. As a percent of total degree completions in 2018, computer science degree completions were roughly 3.2% of the total number of public school degree completions in Texas. This is significantly more than the 2.7% at the peak of the dot-com bubble, especially compared to the increase relative to the post-dot-com bubble low of just 1.2% in 2008. To reach current levels, it required an increase of 2 percentage points between 2008 and 2018. In the decade preceding the dot-com bubble peak, the percentage of computer science degree completions increased by only 1 percentage point!

By contrast, California graduates far more computer science majors than Texas both in levels and as a percentage of degrees awarded. In 2018, computer science degree completions made up 3.7% of all degree completions in California. That is only a half a percentage point higher than the 3.2% of all degree completions at the peak of the dot-com bubble. In other words, Texas has been able to increase the supply of seats more rapidly than they would have had to during the dot-com bubble, and they've done so at the same rate as the home of Silicon Valley, California.

So, although the story of supply shortages might be appealing, an alternative argument has far more to do with students' demand for seats. During the dot-com bubble, states like California and New York exploded into technology hubs. Silicon Valley *needed* tech workers, and it got them. During the run-up to the dot-com bubble, these states had trained many of their own workers, but there was no way that it could supply all of them. So it imported them. Companies trained people to do what they needed. They found uncredentialed workers who had the skills they needed.

Silicon Valley concentrated a large number of like-minded people into one small geographical community. It made computers "cool". Parents who live in the area encouraged their kids to learn about computers and play video games. Companies, in need of workers, donated to local schools for new computers, labs, and after-school programs. In short, the composition of college majors gives us a snapshot of what drives the local economy. It tells us something about what the state needs in terms of workers. In particular, it tells us where a state needs its most talented workers. It lets us know if that state is more likely to innovate or to rent seek.

While all of this is interesting and it is important to establish that there's a reasonable amount of variation across observations, as a researcher, there's nothing provocative in saying that students gravitate toward fields that promise high returns on their investment. However, if we try to label majors as rent seeking related and innovation-related degrees, as Murphy et al. did in their 1991 paper, the findings might prove more provocative.

To start, it's fairly straightforward to categorize innovation-related degrees, degrees that lead to increases in productivity growth. Just as Murphy et al. did, STEM degrees seem to be a safe bet to classify as leading to innovation. Of course, obtaining a STEM degree does not preclude someone from working in a non-STEM field, nor does it preclude someone from working in a STEM field and still rent seeking. However, in the modern economy, significant economic events correspond with significant technological innovation, so it would make sense to say that STEM degrees are, at least on average, innovation-related.

What's somewhat difficult to get right is which degrees are actually STEM degrees. Table 4.1 shows the full list of majors at the two-digit level of the Classification of Instructional Program (CIP). The US Department of Veterans Affairs gives some guidance as to what should be considered a STEM or STEM-related field of study. At the two-digit CIP level of classification, Biological and Biomedical Sciences, Physical Sciences, Science Technologies and Technicians, Computer and Information Science and Support Services, Mathematics and Statistics, Engineering, Engineering Technologies/Technicians, Health Professions and Related Clinical Sciences, Agriculture, Agriculture Operations and Related Sciences, and Natural Resources and Conservation. Within this list, there are a couple of fields that stand out as perhaps not belonging. The most significant of these fields is Health Professions and Related Clinical Sciences. Within that two-digit major field of study, there are a large number of specialties that are not what we might think of as innovation-related and those that require more than a bachelor's degree. In particular, fields like dentistry, nursing, and massage therapy are not what we typically think of as traditional STEM fields of study and health-related degree completions are omitted from the STEM classification.[25]

More difficult still is to correctly classify "rent seeking fields of study". To start, Business, Management, Marketing and Related Support Services and Legal Professions and Studies seem to be a good fit. However, after that, finding support to include a particular field of study is more difficult. An argument could be made to also include social science–degree recipients as a broader indicator of rent seeking. This is because under the social science umbrella are majors like economics and political science that have strong links to business, finance, and government. For this reason, the social science CIP code is considered a rent-seeking-related degree.

After classifying majors as rent-related and STEM-related, we can examine trends in the composition of degree completions as opposed to totals

*Table 4.1* Complete list of majors at the two-digit CIP classification level[26]

| |
|---|
| Agriculture, Agriculture Operations and Related Sciences |
| Architecture and Related Services |
| Area, Ethnic, Cultural and Gender Studies |
| Biological and Biomedical Sciences |
| Business, Management, Marketing and Related Support Services |
| Citizenship Activities |
| Communication, Journalism, and Related Programs |
| Communications Technologies/Technicians and Support Services |
| Computer and Information Sciences and Support Services |
| Construction Trades |
| Education |
| Engineering Technologies/Technicians |
| Engineering |
| English Language and Literature/Letters |
| Family and Consumer Sciences/Human Sciences |
| Foreign Languages, Literatures, and Linguistics |
| Health Professions and Related Clinical Sciences |
| History |
| Legal Professions and Studies |
| Liberal Arts and Sciences, General Studies and Humanities |
| Library Science |
| Mathematics and Statistics |
| Mechanic and Repair Technologies/Technicians |
| Military Technologies |
| Multi/Interdisciplinary Studies |
| Natural Resources and Conservation |
| Parks, Recreation, Leisure and Fitness Studies |
| Personal and Culinary Services |
| Philosophy and Religious Studies |
| Physical Sciences |
| Precision Production |
| Psychology |
| Public Administration and Social Service Professions |
| Science Technologies/Technicians |
| Security and Protective Services |
| Theology and Religious Vocations |
| Transportation and Materials Moving |
| Visual and Performing Arts |

for individual majors. Figure 4.3 shows how the composition of degree completions for public schools changes between 1990 and 2018. Somewhat surprisingly, instead of seeing an uptick in the percentage of STEM-related degrees awarded during the dot-com bubble, we see the opposite. The percentage of STEM-related degrees awarded actually begins to fall before the

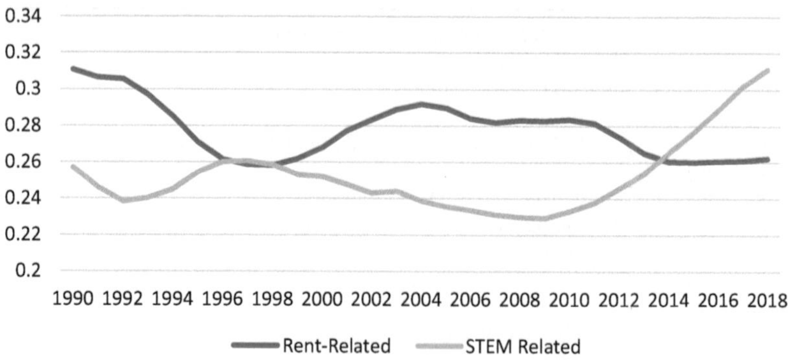


*Figure 4.3* Percentage of public bachelor's degree completions by type for the United States, 1990–2018

Source: Author's calculations using IPEDS.

peak of the dot-com bubble. This suggests that during the dot-com bubble, public school students were more attracted to rent-related fields of study.

It is unclear as to why public colleges and universities graduated fewer STEM-related degrees as a percentage of total graduates during the dot-com bubble. Political rhetoric would suggest that for most states, educating students in STEM fields of study is a high priority. However, political rhetoric did not lead publicly funded colleges and universities to increase the number of STEM students relative to their rent-related peers. This could be because STEM programs have significant capital and staff requirements and that public education systems were unwilling to make that kind of investment across their campuses. Perhaps it is because the returns to rent-related fields were high and the course work was less difficult. Regardless, it is not until post-2014 that the percentage of STEM degree completions exceeds rent-related degree completions through the end of the sample.

These differences point to some possibly interesting policy implications. First, since private schools are notably more expensive than public schools, underserved communities have either less access to or less desire to complete a degree in a STEM-related field. This is problematic for states that are committed to trying to increase the STEM literacy of their workforce as private school graduates are far more likely to work out of state. Second, if state dollars are being spent to train students who will remain in the local workforce, graduating more students with rent-related degrees probably skews tax dollars toward "unproductive" work and away from innovative work.

## Degrees that correlate to economic growth

Figure 4.4[27] shows the correlation between the average state-level growth rate in real personal income per capita from 1990 to 2018 and the percentage of rent-seeking-related-degree completions for public schools by state in 1990. Over this period, the correlation between the composition of rent-related degree completions and state per capita income is negative suggesting that there is a relationship between economic performance and the composition of college graduates.

Furthermore, STEM degree completions in 1990 are positively correlated with the average growth rate of real personal income per capita at the state level between 1990 and 2018 for public schools (Figure 4.5). Again, this suggests that the allocation of talent is correlated with the growth rate of a state, but the causal mechanism is still somewhat unclear.

There are at least two possible channels through which the composition of degree completions could be correlated with the growth rate. The first is the traditional human capital channel, whereby the more students a state graduates with particular skills, the more likely they are to apply those skills on the job. Simply having more students of a particular type makes the state grow faster.

The traditional human capital channel is appealing for a number of reasons. First, it has support in the economic growth literature. For instance, Paul Romer's famous paper on endogenous technological change suggests that simply increasing the human capital stock (in this case, the number of college graduates) would result in an increase in the growth rate.[28] Likewise,

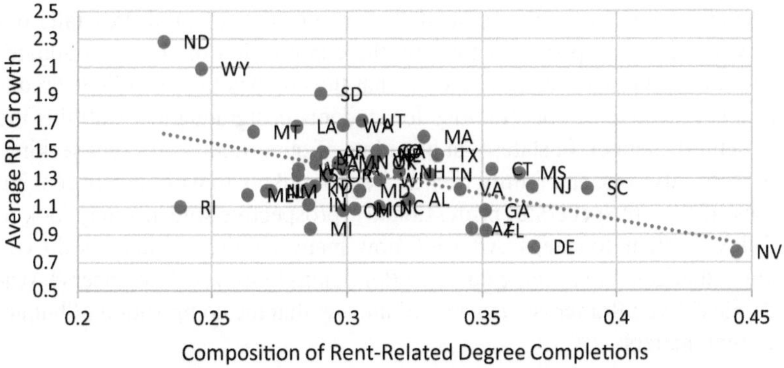


*Figure 4.4* Composition of rent-seeking-related degree completions and the average growth rate of real personal income per capita for public schools

Source: Author's calculations using IPEDS and BEA data.

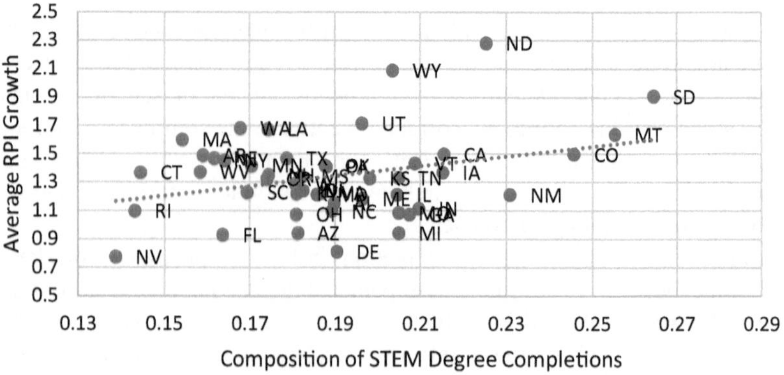


*Figure 4.5* Composition of STEM degree completions and the average growth rate of real personal income per capita for public schools

Source: Author's calculations using IPEDS and BEA data.

Romer argues that the more human capital is devoted to research, the faster the rate of technological innovation and growth. Simply having a larger number of educated people should increase the growth rate. As such, to increase growth, policies should be enacted to make additional schooling more attractive to potential students.

However, this interpretation of causality is not the only one or the most interesting. Of course, most economists would argue that having a more highly educated workforce is good for growth. However, the returns to education may begin declining if the composition of graduates falls out of whack. This explanation for why the composition of college graduates and the growth rate are correlated is that the composition of college graduates is reflective of opportunities for students postgraduation. Call this the structural channel. In states that have lots of opportunities for rent seeking, parents, advisors, and family friends are more likely to work in rent seeking jobs. If they're successful professionally, prospective students may look to follow in their footsteps. After all, how many children of doctors do you know that go on to become doctors? Politicians? Lawyers? Engineers? Academics? Even Romer is cognizant of the fact that the composition of human capital matters:

> If the fundamental policy problem is that we have too many lawyers and MBAs and not enough engineers, a subsidy to physical capital accumulation is a weak, and possibly counterproductive, policy response.[29]

The reason why this is a counterproductive policy response is that in this type of model, capital accumulation is decoupled from investment in research; it does not lead to changes in the growth rate. More research means more innovation means more growth. If there aren't enough researchers, increasing the capital stock will only have level effects and not growth effects. We need our most talented individuals to be innovators, educators, and public servants. As a society, do we really care if we are bad at rent seeking?

More important, if we take the structural approach to human capital, simply throwing money at schools to try to increase the number of graduates may also be a counterproductive policy proposal. Even if the money is earmarked to STEM facilities and to hire STEM faculty, the composition of college graduates may not change. The reason for this is that students have to want to study these programs long before they reach the postsecondary level. They have to see their parents, mentors, and respected members of their communities working in these fields to make them want to train themselves for those fields.

At the national level, this phenomenon is apparent in computer science. The dot-com bubble led students to want to work in that field. However, we should remind ourselves of two important points. First, the response differed by state. Not all states responded to the national computer science boom in the same magnitude because the structure of economies by states varies quite significantly. Second, states have significantly different compositions of degree completions, suggesting that the structure of state economies differ substantially. Finally, even during the dot-com bubble, it's not as though students switched from other fields to STEM fields of study in droves. Most of the inflow into computer science came from other STEM fields. Nationally, the percentage of STEM-related degree completions at public colleges and universities begins to fall long before the peak of the dot-com bubble.

So what is a policymaker to do? For one, they should start by examining the structure of their economies. It is not enough to simply throw money to fund education programs if students are not motivated to pursue them. They should think about whether or not the right types of activities are being rewarded. Are the people who are held up as role models rent seekers? Or are the role models innovators? If the answer to the former is yes, policymakers could start by thinking about how to change incentives around rent seeking.

In particular, policymakers need to stamp out the incentives to rent seeking. From an economic perspective, higher education funding would be better used if it went directly to training students who go on to do things that are socially productive. However, as public colleges and universities rely more and more on tuition and fees, students begin to respond more intensely to their perceived postgraduation career opportunities. If those career prospects are in rent-seeking-related roles, state governments are making irreversible investments that serve to lower, not increase, the social returns to public higher education. To reverse this trend, policymakers must take the prospect of eliminating incentives to rent-seek seriously. How they can do that is the focus of the final chapter.

## Notes

1 For instance, Lucas (1988) defines human capital as the "individual decisions to acquire knowledge, and the consequences of these decisions for productivity". Romer (1990) uses a slightly different definition, "a distinct measure of the cumulative effect of activities such as formal education and on the job training". Lucas, Robert E. (1988). On the Mechanics of Economic Development. *Journal of Monetary Economics, 22*, 3–42; Romer, P. M. (1990). Endogenous Technological Change. *The Journal of Political Economy, 98*(5), S71–S102.

2 Romer (1990); Mankiw, N. G., Romer, D., & Weil, D. N. (1992). A Contribution to the Empirics of Economic Growth. *The Quarterly Journal of Economics, 107*(2), 407–437.

3 Autor, D. H., Katz, L. F., & Kearney, M. S. (2008). Trends in U.S. Wage Inequality: Revising the Revisionists. *The Review of Economics and Statistics, 90*(2), 300–323.

4 Mankiw, Romer, & Weil (1992).

5 US Bureau of Labor Statistics (2019, September 4). Unemployment Rates and Earnings by Educational Attainment. Retrieved from www.bls.gov/emp/chart-unemployment-earnings-education.htm

6 Board of Governors of the Federal Reserve System (US), Student Loans Owned and Securitized, Outstanding [SLOAS]. Retrieved from FRED, Federal Reserve Bank of St. Louis; https://fred.stlouisfed.org/series/SLOAS.

7 Mullainathan, S. (2015, April 10). Why a Harvard Professor Has Mixed Feelings When Students Take Jobs in Finance. *The New York Times*. Retrieved from www.nytimes.com/2015/04/12/upshot/why-a-harvard-professor-has-mixed-feelings-when-students-take-jobs-in-finance.html

8 To be clear, not all finance workers, lawyers, and consultants rent-seek. Many are altruistic and work in roles that pay relatively poorly to advance society.

9 Richardson, James D., ed. (1896). *A Compilation of the Messages and Papers of the Presidents, 1789–1897*. Washington: Published by the authority of Congress, p. 202.

10 Dutt, Amitava, & Veneziani, Roberto (2018). A Classical Model of Education, Growth, and Distribution. *Macroeconomic Dynamics*, 1–36.

11 Of course, calling human capital an "investment" is not the same as economic investment, which gets captured by GDP accounting. Investment, to show up in GDP, requires the purchase of new capital equipment. Since humans are not sold to firms (legally), they would not show up in GDP accounting.

12 Keynes does state investment is revocable for the individual. Once again, there is a tension between societal and individual benefits.

13 The author of this book hated English class.

14 A hypothetical entity that looks to maximize social welfare and ignores individual incentives.

15 Jeffrey, J. (2018, September 1). College Students Say They Want a Degree for a Job. Are They Getting What They Want? *The Washington Post*. Retrieved from www.washingtonpost.com/news/grade-point/wp/2018/09/01/college-students-say-they-want-a-degree-for-a-job-are-they-getting-what-they-want/

16 Johnson, Noel D., LaFountain, Courtney L., & Yamarik, Steven (2011). Corruption Is Bad for Growth (even in the United States). *Public Choice*, *147*(3–4), 3–4; Glaeser, Edward L., & Saks, Raven E. (2006). Corruption in America. *PUBEC Journal of Public Economics*, *90*(6–7), 1053–1072.

17 Magee, Stephen P., Brock, William, & Young, Leslie (1989). *Black Hole Tariffs and Endogenous Policy Theory*. Cambridge University Press.

18 Barro, Robert J. (1991). Economic Growth in a Cross Section of Countries. *The Quarterly Journal of Economics*, *106*(2), 407–443.

19 Murphy, Kevin M., Shleifer, Andrei, & Vishny, Robert W. (1991). The Allocation of Talent: Implications for Growth. *The Quarterly Journal of Economics*, *106*(2), 503–530.

20 This is not to say that computer programmers do not rent-seek or receive rents. Instead, they are more likely to participate in activities that are innovative and drive society forward than someone who works for a financial firm.

21 Title IV institutions of higher education can participate in Title IV Federal Student Aid Programs. To be a title IV school they must be legally allowed to provide postsecondary education in their state, be accredited by a Department of Education–approved accreditation agency, and the Department of Education must certify them to participate in title IV programs. Hegji, A. (2019). Institutional Eligibility for Participation in Title IV Student Financial Aid Programs. CRS Report. Retrieved from https://fas.org/sgp/crs/misc/R43159.pdf

22 Luc Schuster (2016, December 13). In 16 Charts: Higher Education Funding in Massachusetts. *Massachusetts Budget and Policy Center*. Retrieved from https://massbudget.org/report_window.php?loc=higher-education-funding-in-massachusetts.html

23 The percentage of a student's tuition and fees funded by state governments has fallen precipitously nationwide. This is true even in states like Massachusetts, where state funding per resident student has fallen 32% between 2001 and 2018. Thompson, Jeremy (2018, March 1). Educated and Encumbered: Student Debt Rising with Higher Education Funding Falling in Massachusetts. *Massachusetts Budget and Policy Center*. Retrieved from https://massbudget.org/report_window.php?loc=Educated-and-Encumbered.html#chart5

24 US Department of Education, National Center for Education Statistics, Integrated Postsecondary Education Data System (IPEDS), multiple editions, Survey of Institutional Characteristics.

U.S. Department of Education, National Center for Education Statistics, Integrated Postsecondary Education Data System (IPEDS), multiple editions, Survey of Degree Completions.

25 https://benefits.va.gov/gibill/docs/fgib/STEM_Program_List.pdf

26 Not included in the list are Residency Programs, Reserve Officer Training Corps, Personal Awareness and Self-Improvement, Leisure and Recreational Activities, Interpersonal and Social Skills, Basic Skills, Citizenship Activities,

and High School/Secondary Diplomas and Certificates because they are not valid for IPEDS reporting.

27 US Bureau of Economic Analysis (2019). SARPI Real Personal Income by State (accessed January 18, 2020).

28 Romer (1990).

29 Romer (1990), p. S94.

# 5 The politics of removing rents

> I don't think that billionaires should exist, this proposal does not eliminate billionaires, but it eliminates a lot of the wealth that billionaires have, and I think that's exactly what we should be doing.
>
> – Bernie Sanders[1]

Populism is alive and well in the United States. On the left, the rallying cry is behind income and wealth inequality. The rise of political candidates like Bernie Sanders, a self-proclaimed Democratic *Socialist*, speaks to the fact that many Americans, especially young Americans, have reached their outrage constraint. And to be blunt, who can blame them? Strapped with student debt, unable to afford health insurance, and without enough savings to buy a home, many young Americans are experiencing an economy that is not working as well for them as it did for their parents.

Young people's willingness to seemingly overthrow the pure-bred capitalist system in the United States is not irrational. However, the vilification of the exceedingly rich is a bit specious. After all, their greed is founded in our economic system's drive to accumulate wealth. So what is it about today's billionaires that have sparked such outrage?

For one, it's increased awareness. As was mentioned in Chapter 1, economists have dramatically increased the availability of data to the public. The creation of the World Incomes Database and the publication of countless articles and books on the subject have added knowledge to fuel outrage. But one of the breaking points for the American public may have been the Great Recession and the amount of pain that it caused households, the lack of accountability of those on Wall Street, and handouts that went to companies that played a significant role in causing the crisis.

To be clear, this was not the only time major contributors to an economic crisis have been bailed out. In 1970, the federal government bailed out the railroads and consolidated failing companies into Conrail. In the

1980s, the savings-and-loan crisis resulted in large-scale bailouts and regulatory reform. However, the duration and the severity of the economic malaise in the 1980s were not as severe nor as prolonged as the Great Recession. During the savings-and-loan crisis, the headline unemployment rate started increasing from its cyclical low of 5.0% in March 1989, peaked at 7.8% in June 1992, and hit its prerecession low by May 1997.[2] Comparatively, the Great Recession saw the headline unemployment rate increase from 4.4% in May of 2007, peak at 10% in October 2009, and hit a prerecession low in March 2017. The duration of the pain felt by American households was nearly double of that experienced during the savings-and-loan crisis.

However, the larger difference between the two crises might have been the policy response. In total, the savings-and-loan crisis cost $160 billion, $130 billion of which the US government/taxpayers were on the hook for, making the cost far less than the cost of the Great Recession. The total cost of the Great Recession was far larger than just the fiscal stimulus packages provided. The Troubled Asset Relief Program (TARP) authorized $750 billion in spending, which combined with the $831 billion from the American Recovery and Reinvestment Act resulted in a whopping $1.581 trillion of fiscal stimulus.[3] However, looking at just fiscal stimulus only scratches the surface of the total cost of the financial crisis bailout. It's not until looking at the Federal Reserve Bank's balance sheet that we get a full picture of the total cost of the bailout.

In 2007, just prior to the financial crisis, the Federal Reserve had a level of total assets just under $900 billion,[4] 88.45% of which were Treasury securities.[5] Starting in early 2008, the size and structure of the Federal Reserve's balance sheet, and central banks' balance sheets worldwide, changed dramatically. By the end of January 2015, the Federal Reserve's balance sheet expanded to just over $4.5 trillion. Only 54.69% of those assets were Treasury securities. The second-largest line on the Federal Reserve's balance sheet as of January 2015 was the $1.7 trillion in mortgage-backed securities (MBSs) purchased to help sure up a floundering banking system. This puts the total monetary policy cost of the financial crisis at over $3 trillion and the total pledged spending by the US government at roughly $4.5 trillion or about 30% of US gross domestic product.[6]

Aside from the size of the savings-and-loan and Wall Street bailouts, the main difference to the policy response was around holding major players responsible. During the savings-and-loan crisis and its aftermath, there was a strong movement toward holding those associated with the crisis responsible. In 1989, the US government allocated $75 million for the Justice Department through the Financial Institutions Reform, Recovery and

Enforcement Act of 1989 to prosecute financial fraud cases. In total, 616 savings-and-loan-related cases resulted in imprisonment.

Fast-forward to the financial crisis of 2007–2009 and the landscape looks quite different. For the most part, regulators and elected officials agreed that financial market participants acted poorly but that what they did didn't amount to a criminal offense. After all, fraud is a legal term, not a moral one. There are a number of reasons for this, but perhaps the main reason is that during the time leading up to the financial crisis, the adoption of light regulation and little government intervention led to what economist Jim Crotty has dubbed the "New Financial Architecture" (NFA).[7]

Under the NFA, financial markets merged with economic ideology promoting ever laxer regulation. Individuals, acting in their own self-interest should maximize social welfare. As a result of this ideological shift, banks found ways to promote their own self-interests by offering financial products that violated some of the foundations that the NFA architecture was built on. Banks began to issue financial assets that were opaque, illiquid, and impossible to price. Worse still, because of the emphasis placed on private enterprise over the stability of the financial system, banks were essentially left to take any amount of risk that they deemed appropriate, legally.

As a result of the financial crisis of 2007–2009, exactly one banker went to jail in the United States. Kareem Serageldin, a trader for Credit Suisse, was convicted for a conspiracy to falsify books and records and sentenced to 30 months in prison.[8] Meanwhile, banks have been fined a total of $243 billion for their role in the financial crisis for misleading investors around the riskiness of mortgages used to create the MBSs and their derivatives that nearly destroyed global financial markets.

In my estimation, it is this fact, that almost nobody was truly held accountable for the financial crisis while millions suffered, that finally pushed American politics to the breaking point. So where better to start with the shifting political landscape than the financial markets?

## Banks acting badly

The causes and consequences of the financial crisis of 2007–2009 and the Great Recession are well documented. Prolonged economic expansion and a housing boom led to increased risk-taking by financial institutions. The risk-taking was amplified by the securitization of mortgages into MBSs. Out of these MBSs came a market for an endless array of derivatives and financial instruments such as credit-default swaps. When the economy started to slow, unemployment rates began to rise, and home prices began to fall, causing the securities based on those underlying assets (mortgages) to lose value as well. As liquidity in the MBS market and their derivatives dried up, the financial crisis was in full swing.

The preceding story of the financial crisis told is also a story that fits nicely within the context of rent seeking, especially if you look at it through the lens of being an activity that is profitable for the individual but does not produce any output as a result. Even worse, the actions taken by the financial system were extremely costly to society as a whole. To be clear, the individual incentives from the MBS and MBS-related instruments were monumental. Between 2003 and 2007, it is estimated that banks generated nearly $2 trillion in fees associated with the securitization of mortgages. As a result, banks paid their executives and workers billions of dollars' worth of bonuses that did not have to be paid back when the market for these innovative securities and derivatives crumbled.[9]

At this point, it's worth taking a step back and thinking about what the role of financial intermediaries is in an economy. As an individual, I am capable of managing my own financial portfolio, albeit poorly. The primary reason financial intermediaries exist is to help manage risk and financial intermediaries are indeed better suited to manage risk than any individual. As mentioned in Chapter 2, they are professionals with access to vast troves of data, large numbers of highly trained and educated employees, and the ability to pool money and diversify across a large number of assets.

However, at certain points in time, their knowledge about the trade-offs between risk and reward can put financial firms in a precarious spot. They know that the less risky an asset is, the lower its return. That's one of the reasons why US government debt pays such low interest rates; it's the risk-free rate. The riskier the debt instrument, the higher the interest rate is, but the more likely the bet is to go bad and leave the financial investor with nothing. So the holy grail is to find an asset that has high returns but has a low risk of default.

Of course, nothing like this actually exists. The return on an asset is largely determined by its risk profile. However, in the lead-up to the financial crisis, MBSs were considered by ratings agencies to be AAA-rated and therefore low risk. However, these same MBSs had higher average returns than other AAA-rated assets. How could this be true? One possibility is that it wasn't. Looking at the ex post performance of MBSs leading into the financial crisis, it is clear that credit-rating agencies and financial market participants grossly underestimated the level of risk.

Research by the Federal Reserve supports this theory. In the final years leading up to the financial crisis, MBSs that received a AAA rating from credit agencies became riskier as they possessed a larger percentage of low-quality mortgages.[10] Looking at this from the perspective of Minsky's Financial Instability Hypothesis,[11] this makes perfect sense. During long periods of tranquility, market participants tend to become overly optimistic, take on even more risk, and sow the seeds for their own demise.

Rent seeking also plays a role in this story. One of the big driving forces leading to the increase in riskiness of MBSs is that market participants have what Crotty refers to as perverse incentives. High-level executives, or what he refers to as "Rainmakers", have incentives to increase risk in the short term to maximize returns because once they receive their compensation, they do not have to give it back. For the financial system, this holds even at the institutional level because banks know that they are systemically important.[12] Again, this is rent seeking as increased risk benefits the individual and can lead to negative consequences for the firm and economy as a whole.

As a result of banks, in particular individuals within a bank, taking on excessive amounts of risk to try to capture excess returns, policymakers looked to limit how much an individual's compensation could be tied to current performance. Within the Dodd–Frank Wall Street Reform and Consumer Protection Act, there is a set of provisions on executive compensation. As written, the Dodd–Frank Act requires that publicly traded financial institutions give shareholders a nonbinding say on executive compensation and golden parachutes.[13]

In addition to having provisions on shareholder pay, it also includes a provision for executive compensation clawbacks. This requires that the company disclose policies related to incentive-based compensation and how pay awarded during the previous three-year period can be clawed back if there is a restatement for any reason. Unfortunately (from the perspective of limiting incentives to rent-seek), as of 2018, the clawback provision has yet to be implemented by the Securities and Exchange Commission.

## Speed trap

Thomas Petterfy's rubber hands laid the groundwork for what would become the ever more complex and increasingly capital-intensive industry of high-frequency trading. As time has gone on, the benefits of high-frequency trading have been called into question by market participants and politicians alike. In the wake of the financial crisis that has painted all of Wall Street as villains and following an increase in the frequency of market "flash crashes", a number of policies have been proposed to try to curb the speed and prevalence of highly sophisticated trading outfits on the financial markets.

A financial-transactions tax is one such way that policymakers could try to curb the number of transactions made by financial market participants. The intent of such a tax is to curb speculation and decrease volatility. Financial-transactions taxes are nothing new, Keynes proposed a financial-transactions tax in the wake of the Great Depression. He envisioned it as a way of trying to make speculation so expensive that it would reduce its frequency much like "casinos should, in the public interest, be inaccessible and expensive".[14]

Since then, with the support of some economists, a number of politicians have proposed some sort of financial-transactions tax of varying severity since the financial crisis. The names of the proposals do not hold back their animosity toward Wall Street. The "Let Wall Street Pay for the Restoration of Main Street Act of 2009" proposes a tax on a number of different types of securities transactions with tax exemptions for retirement accounts, health savings accounts, educational accounts, regulated investment companies, and individuals (up to $500 per married couple). Half of the tax revenue raised would be put into a "Job Creation Reserve", and the other half would be used to pay down the deficit.[15] Both of these items were viewed as ways to solve the unique problems that resulted from the financial crisis, namely, soaring unemployment and a soaring deficit.

Similarly, nongovernment proposals such as the "Robin Hood Tax" have been endorsed by more than 150 organizations, including student groups, unions, economists, and policy think tanks. Just like the "Let Wall Street Pay" tax, the "Robin Hood Tax" proposes a sub–one percentage point tax on securities transactions. The major difference is what the tax intends to pay for. Instead of being used to help pay down the deficit, the "Robin Hood Tax" would devote all its revenues to paying for hiring workers, reducing foreclosures, increasing access to health care, feeding low-income Americans, expanding research and development, and fighting climate change – essentially, a liberal wish list.[16]

Of course, there has been no financial-transactions tax implemented in the United States since the financial crisis. Resistance on the part of conservatives against government intervention in the marketplace, as well as concerns of reduced liquidity in the financial markets, have quashed these efforts. Interest in a financial-transactions tax has increased among the Democratic 2020 presidential candidates, including Senator Bernie Sanders, who had cosponsored financial-transactions taxes in 2009,[17] 2011,[18] and 2013,[19] Elizabeth Warren, who cosponsored a financial-transactions tax in 2019,[20] and Tulsi Gabbard, who cosponsored a financial-transactions tax in 2019.[21] Even Wall Street billionaire Michael Bloomberg is backing a financial-transactions tax as part of his platform. Although Democratic front-runner Joe Biden has verbally endorsed a financial-transactions tax, it cannot be found in writing.

What is clear about all the proposals is that a financial-transactions tax is seen as a way of trying to limit a social bad, what this book defines as rent seeking, in the hope of funding something that is for the social good. In the case of Elizabeth Warren, that means using the money to finance her Medicare for All plan. Bernie Sanders proposes using the financial-transactions tax to raise $2.4 trillion to pay for higher education by cancelling all student debt and making public colleges, universities, Historically Black Colleges and Universities, Minority-Serving Institutions, and trade schools free for everyone.[22]

Economists and policy wonks disagree on many of the details of each candidate's proposed plans. They argue about how much it would actually cost to provide public higher education over the next decade and how much money each plan would actually raise. However, what economists do agree on is that taxing social bads and subsidizing social goods is good economic policy. This is because even with well-functioning markets, there is always the prospect of negative externalities.

Rent seeking is actually a market distortion. The goal of policy should be to make it so that rent seeking strategies in the financial markets are not profitable and eliminated. Policies that are specifically designed to raise money off those activities, in a sense, miss the point. Sure, it's noble that we want to find a way to pay for more affordable health care and higher education,[23] but why would we want to rely on maintaining a certain level of unproductive activity to achieve it?

Instead, policymakers should focus on eliminating the market distortions caused by rent seeking altogether by banning certain types of market behaviors or participants. Let's consider the problem of firms investing in reducing latency. Instead of taxing firms, why not put limits on the technology market participants can use to access stock market data feeds? This would be similar to mandating that NASCAR race cars all race the same car[24] or that Thomas Peterffy's traders have to execute their stock trades by hand.

The purpose of this is to stifle socially wasteful innovation. Of course, I don't think anyone would argue that technologies that improve market efficiency are socially wasteful. However, technologies that may, at best, marginally improve market efficiency but come at enormous cost should be curtailed. It's hard to imagine that spending hundreds of millions of dollars on fiber optic cables to shave a few microseconds off the amount of time it takes to execute a trade benefits society whatsoever. It's easy to imagine that spending that money on things with positive externalities, like most public goods, society would be unequivocally better off.

## Targeting past rents

The rich have become fertile targets for left-leaning politicians who, armed with data on the runaway levels of income and wealth inequality, have started to shift the rhetoric from the fairness of the labor market to striking concerns about equity. Much of this shift has been driven by the ability of the wealthiest individuals to escape the financial crisis of 2007–2009 essentially unscathed and the ability for high-income individuals to keep their earnings even as their companies laid off workers or failed.

The experience of lower-income Americans was very different. The unemployment rates of nonsupervisory employees, minorities, and non-credentialed workers increased significantly compared to more financially secure counterparts, on average. Of course, wealthy individuals felt some pain during the downturn itself. As equity markets, real estate values, and credit defaults take hold during a crisis, wealth decreases dramatically. However, during expansions, wealth tends to lead and declines in unemployment tend to follow. In the medium run, the wealthy simply feel less pain. For low-wealth individuals having no income but maintaining financial obligations, it is catastrophic as it may lead to their insolvency.

These differentiated experiences contributed to post Great Recession attitudes toward wealthy people. How is it possible that people who have contributed greatly to the prolonged economic malaise get off relatively unscathed while those who bore the brunt of the downturn receive little to no assistance? After all, large financial institutions and investors received trillions of dollars' worth of bailout money to deal with price declines in MBSs caused by increases in the rate of foreclosures of the underlying assets. Meanwhile, homeowners, whose ability to pay their mortgages determines the rate of foreclosures, were left without support.

The anger around the ill-gotten gains, the rents, captured by those at the top spilled over into the political sphere. For conservatives, especially, the thought of government bailouts violated their economic ideology and raised questions of moral hazard. Firms and investors that behave badly should be allowed to fail through the tenets of economic Darwinism. Liberals, aligned with some sort of New Keynesian doctrine, understood the need for the government to step in and spend money but abhorred the idea of bailing out Wall Street without substantial support headed to "Main Street".

Deeply concerned about moral hazard, politicians have looked to find ways to claw back what they perceive as ill-gotten gains and distribute them to Main Street. One policy that has gained serious traction among progressive politicians and economists is a wealth tax. The argument is that income taxes might be enough to disincentivize current rent seeking behavior but by implementing a wealth tax you could capture and redistribute previous rents. There are reasons why such a wealth tax could make sense.

Consider an example. Imagine that the average American wanted to increase their wealth. How would they do it? For most, they would try to save some money out of their current income. Say, 10% per year of their *after-tax* income is a reasonable goal for most. For the median household, which took home $63,179 pretax in 2018,[25] that means that they would try to save, on average, roughly $5,891.10.[26] This would be the contribution to this household's wealth. Had they been able to save out of their pretax income, they would've been able to contribute $6,317.90. Essentially, having to pay tax on their flow of current income costs this household $426.80 or 6.8% of the contribution to their wealth![27]

However, imagine that you are an ultra-wealthy household with most of your net worth tied up in business interests. Sure, your company pays corporate tax, maybe, and you may pay more in taxes than your average American counterparts (if you earn an income at all), but you do not have to pay tax on your current wealth increases. Instead, because your assets are already in the form of wealth, any accrual to that value is untaxed until sold. A person with a net worth of $1 billion earning a very modest 2% return on their investments would have their wealth increase by $20,000,000, and that contribution to their wealth is tax-free. The $20 million is essentially tax-free income.

Since the Great Recession, elected officials on the left have pushed strongly for the implementation of a wealth tax. Elizabeth Warren's "Ultra-Millionaire" wealth tax proposal looks to levy a progressive 2% annual tax on the net worth of households above $50 million and 6% on the net worth of households above $1 billion. Over a ten-year period, her wealth tax would generate estimated revenues of roughly $3.75 trillion.[28] Bernie Sanders's proposed "Tax on Extreme Wealth" calls for a progressive tax of 1% tax on wealth of households with a net worth over $32 million and increases by wealth bracket to a maximum of 8% on wealth over $10 billion. His plan would raise an estimated $4.35 trillion over the next 10 years and cut the wealth of billionaires in half over 15 years.[29] Joe Biden does not have a plan to implement a wealth tax.

Although a wealth tax is a predominantly liberal idea, back in 1999, Donald Trump proposed a radical wealth tax while running for the Reform Party's presidential nomination. His wealth tax was designed to pay off the government's debt, not to fund new social programs. The proposed tax was to be a one-time flat tax of 14.25% on individuals and trusts with a net worth of over $10 million and would have raised $5.7 trillion.[30] This would have been nearly enough to pay off the entire $5.8 trillion national debt held by the United States in the fourth quarter of 1999.[31]

Regardless of the source, wealth taxes, such as the ones outlined earlier, should be relatively popular. After all, in 2014 the wealthiest 1% of households averaged "only" $18.92 million of wealth.[32] This means that more than 99% of the population would not have their tax liability increase whatsoever and, depending on how the money was used, would actually see either their tax liabilities or expenses decrease. Recent polls have found support for a wealth tax with 64% of respondents supporting the idea that "the very rich should contribute an extra share of their total wealth each year to support public programs".[33]

From a rent seeking perspective, a wealth tax would make a certain amount of sense as it would allow for the government to capture past rents from private coffers and spend them on programs with high social returns. However, this type of policy does little to disincentivize current rent seeking without significant income tax reform. In a sense, past damage is done, and although wealth disparities bring about a sense of unfairness, on their own, they do not cause social harm.[34] But as we saw during the lead up to the Great Recession, the real risks from rent seeking play out in the present and aren't always realized until a later date.

As is true with any government intervention, a wealth tax would be difficult to implement, at least in part, due to the ability of wealthy individuals to craft schemes to avoid paying taxes. The Warren and Sanders plans both outline ways to try to limit tax avoidance by increasing funding and audit rates for the Internal Revenue Service (IRS) and promising to enact a 40% "exit tax" on households that try to avoid paying the tax by renouncing their citizenship or moving their wealth overseas. Even with these provisions in place, increased regulation and taxation has the potential to lead to an uptick in rent seeking as impacted parties with enough to lose end up paying substantial sums of money just to avoid paying the tax. Tax avoidance is another form of rent seeking.

The most difficult part of implementing a wealth tax would be collection. Many high-net-worth individuals hold their assets in something other than cash. The wealthiest 1% of households hold a very small percentage of their assets in the form of cash, meaning that in order to make wealth tax payments, they would have to sell assets of differing levels of liquidity. This could have a significant impact on asset prices.

According to the Federal Reserve's Survey of Consumer Finances,[35] as net worth increases, the percentage of illiquid assets also increases, with the largest asset class being "business interests" once a household's net worth exceeds $10 million. If the "business interests" are in privately held companies, much of the owner's wealth may be extremely illiquid.[36] Of course, high-net-worth individuals also hold a substantial portion of their wealth in the form of stocks and mutual funds, which can be transformed into cash quickly to pay their wealth tax, but it may also have a significant negative impact on equity values. For instance, if the entirety of the wealth tax proposed by Bernie Sanders, $4.53 trillion, were to be paid for through the sale of US equities, it would be equivalent to roughly half of the $9.07 trillion loss in direct and indirect stock holdings by US households between the third quarter of 2007 and the first quarter of 2009.[37] Half of a financial crisis!

Not all assets are as easy to price and sell as US equities and business interests. Fine art, large homes, fast cars, and complex arrays of businesses would make auditing wealthy individuals extremely challenging. Even with a designated "Wealth Squad", the audit of a single billionaire could take years, potentially turn up next to nothing, and contribute to rent seeking as wealthy individuals employ teams of lawyers to ensure their clients pay as little as possible back to the IRS.[38] Increasing the number of audits, particularly for high-net-worth individuals, would likely further feed the tax-avoidance industry.

Proposals for wealth taxes have not come solely from politicians. More liberal economists have also proposed wealth taxes to help reign in the runaway wealth concentration of the rich. In Emmanuel Saez and Gabriel Zucman's recent book, they propose a modest wealth tax of 2% on wealth above $50 million and 3.5% on wealth above $1 billion to ensure that extremely wealthy individuals pay taxes and to slow the dramatic increase in wealth inequality.[39]

But this is not a story about how unfair the tax system is and how the ultra-wealthy have been able to game it.[40] Instead, it's about what to do about past rents and the argument of a wealth tax to stomp out rent seeking is unconvincing. Instead of taxing past rents, we should be more concerned with making sure that rents don't accumulate in the first place, and this requires a vigorously progressive income tax. As we have seen throughout this book, rent seeking is most rewarding when the stakes for the individual are high. Successful rent seeking concentrates gains among the hands of the very few, which eventually leads to wealth inequality.

So, if you want to stomp out wealth inequality, you have to stomp out current rents and that involves finding ways to curtail rent seeking. Implementing a team of IRS agents to try to audit high-net-worth individuals annually will certainly raise additional tax revenues for the country. However, it will also be fertile ground for rent seeking. Teams of lawyers, producing only lawyering services, will get paid handsomely to minimize the taxes on the wealthy. This is hardly beneficial from a social welfare perspective.

## Stomping out trolls

Patents provide inventors with exclusive rights to bring their intellectual property to market for a defined period. In a sense, it provides the owner of the patent exclusive rights to monopoly rents where, in this case, the rents themselves are seen as a reward for the production of a new idea that is a social good. Sure, for the defined amount of time that the patent is valid, the market for that patent will be inefficient, but if it truly is a marketable idea, society as a whole will be better off for having that product exist. In theory, that's why policymakers allow for patents to exist.

And there is a case to be made that patents may be socially beneficial through at least four channels. They may motivate invention, induce the necessary capital to finance taking an idea to market, allow inventors to disclose ideas, and prevent stepping on toes.[41] The first channel is the most commonly cited. Proponents of this channel suggest that in order to bring inventions to market, they need some sort of legal protection against duplication. This is because the research and development costs of a new product can be extensive and incurred almost exclusively by the inventing party. The second channel builds off the first, because patents are usually awarded long before the product is commercially viable. Patent protection allows the inventor protection while they continue the path towards commercialization.

The remaining two channels are less commonly cited. Where patent laws do not exist, or where they are not strong, companies rely on secrecy to keep others from stealing their innovations.[42] This prevents the dissemination of knowledge that could be useful for other firms and made accessible through licensing of the patent. The dissemination and sharing of knowledge lead to the final channel by ensuring that researchers do not end up redeveloping existing ideas because secrecy prevents market participants from knowing that ideas they are researching already exist. These two channels are similar to those outlined by Paul Romer,[43] and the extensive endogenous growth literature followed. These channels suggest that by having strong patent laws, the dissemination of knowledge would increase the ability of researchers to "stand on the shoulders" of other researchers. The "fishing out" effect would be limited because researchers would not waste time trying to reinvent the wheel.[44]

However, the dangerous side of patents is the rents that they create are ripe for the taking. It is the very existence of rents that builds an entire industry around capturing them. The inventor, the owner of the idea, be it an individual or firm, becomes the target for a number of rent seekers. There are the businesspeople who promise to maximize profit for a cut even though the value that they add may be questionable. There are competitors who copy the technology illegally and dare the inventor to sue them. There are companies worried about losing market share with teams of lawyers set to argue in court that the idea is not novel or that it is obvious, even if it is completely new and obscure. There are also a number of people who look to file blocking patents to either block a new and innovative product from coming to market, like patenting a machine or process that needs to be used in the production of a particular good or intentionally filing patents that are not novel or not obvious. These types of patents if approved are potentially destructive to entire industries, especially if the patent holder never has any interest in bringing the product to market.

Seemingly countless dollars are spent and hours upon hours are wasted on depositions and in courts, where companies' lawyers fight over patents in hopes of being able to protect their rents or eliminate their competition's rents. It is precisely because courts are willing to overturn patents that they are worth fighting over. If courts were unwilling to overturn patent rights, the legal challenges would stop altogether.

One possible solution to eliminating wasteful patent litigation is to make the original patent permanent. Once the US Patent Office issues a patent, that patent protects the patent holder from not only competition but also legal challenges. Of course, this raises rent seeking problems of its own. The number of patent filings may increase dramatically with a large number of them being invalid, as they are not novel or nonobvious, and hoping for approval or are valid but designed to block competition. In each case, fees would be paid to patent offices, lawyers would likely be hired to make sure the paperwork was filed correctly, and firms would monitor the marketplace to make sure that no one infringes on their patents. This is still rent seeking behavior. It serves to be extremely profitable at the individual level while not producing any output.

Indeed, US lawmakers have reignited the political debate on patent strength, in large part, due to the increased prevalence of patent trolls. The "Support Technology and Research for Our Nation's Growth and Economic Resilience (STRONGER) Patents Act", which was most recently reintroduced to the House of Representatives in the summer of 2019 by Steve Stivers and 22 cosponsors, flouts the perceived social benefits of patents and proposes to strengthen the patent holders' "property rights". The language in the bill restates the claim that patents are "an essential part of the country's economic success" and that "strong patent rights encourage United States inventors to invest their resources in creating new inventions".[45]

The bill's primary purpose of strengthening patent rights is to make it more difficult for awarded patents to be overturned by the legal system, thus making the patents stronger by placing the burden of proof on the challenger to clearly out the "unpatentability of a previously issued claim by clear and convincing evidence".[46] Seemingly, this bill is designed to stomp out patent trolls, or nonpracticing entities (NPEs), whose aim is to use litigation to capture rents by challenging the validity of a patent holder's property rights.

But it's unclear if stronger patents will actually have their desired effect of fostering innovation. Economic research has produced a wide array of papers examining whether or not stronger patent protections actually lead to increased innovation. Research out of the St. Louis Federal Reserve Bank puts it bluntly in the first line of a widely cited paper, "there is no empirical evidence that they serve to increase innovation and productivity, unless the latter is identified with the number of patents awarded".[47] They go on to provide evidence from the existing literature that indeed, stronger patents and reduced competition do not lead to increased productivity, even though they do lead to an increase in the number of patents. Given the theoretical mechanisms through which patents should stimulate innovation and, therefore, productivity growth, this leads us to a patent puzzle. How can a policy thoughtfully designed to foster innovation actually hinder it?

The answer is simple: rent seeking. In an ideal setting, patents would be awarded only for nonobvious and novel ideas that are used to advance the knowledge and well-being of humankind. However, it is becoming increasingly common that patents have been used to stifle competition and capture rents. NPEs file large numbers of patents that they never intend on using. Clearly, this is not the intent of patent law. Unfortunately, it is the consequence. To make matters worse, the STRONGER Patents Act looks to strengthen the rights of patent holders, incentivizing NPEs to stockpile even more idle patents in the hope of forcing producing firms to pay licensing fees. Without a simultaneous increase in the requirements for obtaining a patent, it is likely that NPEs will try to increase their questionable patent holdings and reduce the overall quality of patents issued.[48]

The current state of patent law in the United States is to facilitate more rent seeking than innovation. A well-functioning patent market should induce innovation barring negative rent seeking behavior. However, it appears that in a developed economy like the United States, the allure of rent seeking has served to counteract its benefits and that the patent system, as it exists, is serving to stifle innovation and productivity growth.

The strengthening of patent holder's rights is, therefore, more of a result of American political ideology than evidence. The American inventor is, to a certain extent, at the heart of the American Dream. Without substantial patent protections, a substantial part of the American Dream dies. However, when ideology contradicts evidence, it's time to start thinking about a way out of an antiquated system.

At the extreme, the patent system could be abolished. This would undoubtedly increase competition among producers. Firms would have to rely on secrecy to keep from having competitors replicate their innovations. However, abolishing the patent system altogether may have disastrous consequences in industries without the potential for product differentiation and where replication is relatively easy.

Research and development–intensive industries, such as pharmaceuticals, chemicals, and manufacturing, may require some sort of intellectual property protection as with today's technology, it is possible for firms to replicate products and production processes quickly. This could be particularly harmful to society as advancement in medicine is squarely aligned with social welfare.

This puts policymakers between a rock and a hard place. We need a robust pharmaceutical industry with sufficient incentives to ensure that new drugs are created to deal with the ever-evolving health needs of humanity. It is well known that there are positive externalities associated with things like vaccines, suggesting that they are undersupplied in the marketplace. However, granting monopoly power to a firm results in the underproduction of that good, below the competitive market-equilibrium quantity. In cases where there are positive externalities, even the competitive market-equilibrium quantity is below the socially optimal quantity.

The potential damage to society from restricting competition for pharmaceuticals is that lifesaving drugs may exist but be prohibitively expensive. Even though its patent had expired, Daraprim, a drug used to treat a severe infection caused by *Toxoplasma gondii*,[49] saw its price increase from $13.50 to $750 overnight.[50] The now-infamous "Pharma Bro" price hike drew outrage from politicians and the Infectious Disease Society of America as it significantly restricted access to lifesaving treatment for people who are immunocompromised from HIV and treatments for cancer.

Elsewhere, government-run health systems are left in a precarious situation as they are forced to decide whether to pay for expensive medications protected by patents. This is especially true for drugs used to treat rare diseases or "orphan drugs". Whether countries are willing to provide the treatments depends on a number of factors, including "the severity of the disease, If the treatment will provide health gain, rather than just stabilisation of the condition [and] if the disease is life threatening".[51]

If governments can make decisions about what lifesaving treatments to give to patients, they surely can make more nuanced decisions about whether an idea qualifies for a patent. With this in mind, we might begin pondering what an optimal patent system might look like. Governments, instead of awarding patents based on their novelty and nonobviousness, should look to award patents to inventors and companies for ideas that would increase social welfare by disseminating useful information, bring new products to market, and establish intellectual property in situations only where replication would be simple.

Another fairly simple way to help solve the patent problem would be to award patents contingent on the underlying idea being brought to market within a given time frame. This ensures that patent aggregators cannot simply compile blocking patents to prevent competition. It also allows for the dissemination of knowledge so that if a company cannot figure out a way to bring the idea to market, the patent protection expires and another firm can try to execute the now publicly available idea. A second production patent could be awarded to companies to protect their intellectual property for a certain timeframe once they've created a viable product. This protects, albeit in a modified way, the rewards channels for inventors while limiting incentives for patent trolls.

But what about those pesky pharmaceutical companies who produce products that are expensive in terms of their research and development due to intense regulation, are easily replicated, and provide significant social benefits? This type of product may need to fall under a different type of patent application. Since pharmaceuticals with high social benefits are undersupplied by private markets, the government could fund research and development for certain products and allow companies to produce their generics without patent protection. Alternatively, private research and development could continue unfunded but the company could apply for cost reimbursement for clinical trials in exchange for drug companies offering the drug at regulated prices.[52]

Regardless of the solution, it is clear that the patent system in the United States is broken as there is a lack of empirical evidence suggesting that patents foster innovation and productivity growth. Simply strengthening property rights of patent holders does not eliminate the costs of rent seeking associated with the US patent system. That does not mean that the theoretical channels through which patents *could* foster innovation and productivity growth are unfounded. Rather, in the face of rent seeking strategies, patents should be redesigned in such a way that they place social welfare ahead of rents.

## Conclusion

This book tried to accomplish four sweeping goals. First, it tried to offer a clear definition of rent seeking that was specific, but not limited, to the public sphere. Second, it tried to use examples of how rent seekers can capture rents outside of the public sphere. Third, it tried to suggest that a high concentration of rent seekers can have negative growth effects at the state level. Finally, it gave some examples of how attitudes towards rent seeking have infiltrated the policy discussion of the United States. The hope is not that this is a definitive work on the subject of rent seeking. Instead, my hope is that this book contributes to building a broader discussion on the topic of private rent seeking and the economy.

Without seriously considering the consequences of rent seeking, I fear that economists set themselves far too easy a task. Not all "production" is created equal. In fact, much of what occurs in a predominately service-based economy can fall victim to rampant rent seeking. Note that in every example outlined earlier, the production of a physical good is never rent seeking. Instead, it's the executive lobbying for resources, the chief executive officer influencing their own compensation package, the stock trader taking excessive risk, and the lawyers defending and challenging claims to intellectual property rights. It is not the worker making a widget, although it might be the worker trying to conceive ways to get away with shirking duties of widget-making.

Although these activities may contribute to personal accumulation, they do little, if anything, to contribute to social accumulation. In fact, the suggestive evidence in Chapter 4 suggests the opposite is true. Rent seeking, fighting over the proceeds from already-realized production, leads economies to accumulate less as they waste otherwise productive resources. This is an inefficiency that should be addressed by economists of all types. Just because there is a market for something and people are willing and able to pay a high price doesn't make it an efficient use of resources.

Instead, economists should set a course to maximize social welfare by acknowledging that, at the macro level, markets can lead to an inefficient allocation of resources. This does not mean that there are not benefits from occupations that have a potential to lead to rent seeking. No sane economist would argue that because some people who work on Wall Street rent-seek, we should abolish the financial markets. Instead, a nuanced understanding of rent seeking suggests that extremely high returns should come with high taxes because abnormal returns rarely, if ever, are truly a reward to superior skill. Instead, they are a reward to their ability to make monetary claims on their contribution, which would be impossible to claim on activities with broad social benefits.

Perhaps the most concerning consequence of rent seeking is that occupations with large social contributions are being starved. Teachers, social workers, public servants, and production workers, among others, have all seen their incomes decline relative to rent seekers. In an efficient labor market, the most talented individuals will pursue careers in fields that have the highest returns. As a result, our public servants are less adept and our teachers are less talented. It's fair to say that society would be better off if our best and brightest were working toward the public good as opposed to their own private benefit.

What are we to do? The simplest way to stomp out rent seeking would be to curb the returns to rent seeking. Extraordinarily high incomes should be taxed at extraordinarily high tax rates. Governments should reimplement highly progressive income taxes that approach 100% for the highest-income earners. Critics, of course, will argue that high income tax rates will reduce incentives to innovate. After all, it's the profit motive that drives innovation.

I would argue that this is not true from a social perspective. Those people who are motivated solely by the profit motive will be more inclined to rent seek and do not usually make for good social stewards. For example, faculty members who produce research for monetary gain are likely to be disappointed. Excellent faculty members produce research to satisfy their intellectual curiosity and further public knowledge, regardless of the private returns.

However, we need to be cognizant that any government willing to try to alter the relative income distribution exposes itself to new rent seeking schemes. The prospect of paying higher taxes may cause high-income households to hide overseas, develop creative accounting measures, and set off a team of lobbyists to negotiate loopholes for their clients. In effect, the government itself rent seeks as it tries to capture existing rents for its own coffers. The good news is, that if the government is successful in reducing rent seeking, not simply making money off the rent seekers, there will be fewer resources to challenge the government intervention in the long run.

The focus on public goods has never been more important than it is today. At the time of this writing, the world finds itself mired in a global pandemic. Faced with the prospect of wide-scale loss of life, governments in developed countries have elected to essentially shutter their economies. In response, governments have been overwhelmingly willing to pass highly progressive policies. In the United States, the government has agreed to finance $2.2 trillion worth of payments that includes generous unemployment benefits that replace nearly 100% of most workers' incomes, a payment of $2,400 per household and $500 per child for couples making under $150,000 per year, and billions of dollars' worth of loans to small businesses that turn into grants if they keep workers on the payroll. In addition, US health insurers have agreed to waive copays for testing related to the pandemic.

The Coronavirus Aid, Relief, and Economic Security (CARES) Act was passed by a deeply divided US House of Representatives and Senate with hardly any controversy. Unlike the government bailout during the financial crisis, there have been no cries of moral hazard, nearly no discussion of the ballooning government debt, and no threat of a veto from a president who promised to pay down the national debt.

In addition, there has been a race to develop treatment and a vaccine for COVID-19. Partially funded by the government, research universities and pharmaceutical companies have devoted vast resources to try to stop the spread of the disease and hopefully eradicate it from the planet. The incredible advances in science will likely allow for a vaccine to be produced in the relatively near future.

Imagine, for a moment, if the normal rules of supply and demand were to apply to this scenario. People, scared of the consequences of getting a novel disease, would likely be willing to pay the equivalent to a small fortune to protect themselves. If the vaccine were protected under a patent, the developing company could demand monopoly prices. Individual protection, however, isn't the point. The point of a vaccine is to develop a social immunity to a disease to protect society against wide-scale loss of life and overwhelmed hospital systems and to decrease reliance on nonpharmaceutical interventions, allowing economies to reopen. Hopefully, pharmaceutical companies will put society first and forgo collecting rents.

The rest of society should follow suit.

## Notes

1 Kaplan, Thomas (2019, September 24). Bernie Sanders Proposes a Wealth Tax: "I Don't Think That Billionaires Should Exist". *The New York Times*. Retrieved from www.nytimes.com/2019/09/24/us/politics/bernie-sanders-wealth-tax.html
2 US Bureau of Labor Statistics, Unemployment Rate [UNRATE]. Retrieved from FRED, Federal Reserve Bank of St. Louis; https://fred.stlouisfed.org/series/UNRATE (accessed March 17, 2020).
3 It should be noted that not all of the TARP money was spent and that the federal government received more in repayments than they spent to shore up businesses.
4 Board of Governors of the Federal Reserve System (US). Assets: Total Assets: Total Assets (Less Eliminations from Consolidation): Wednesday Level [WALCL]. Retrieved from FRED, Federal Reserve Bank of St. Louis; https://fred.stlouisfed.org/series/WALCL (accessed March 17, 2020).
5 Board of Governors of the Federal Reserve System (US). Assets: Securities Held Outright: U.S. Treasury Securities: Bills: Wednesday Level [WSHOBL]. Retrieved from FRED, Federal Reserve Bank of St. Louis; https://fred.stlouisfed.org/series/WSHOBL (accessed March 17, 2020).
6 US Bureau of Economic Analysis, Gross Domestic Product [GDP]. Retrieved from FRED, Federal Reserve Bank of St. Louis; https://fred.stlouisfed.org/series/GDP (accessed March 17, 2020).
7 Crotty, James (2009, July). Structural Causes of the Global Financial Crisis: A Critical Assessment of the "New Financial Architecture". *Cambridge Journal of Economics*, *33*(4), 563–580.

8 Noonan, Laura, Tilford, Cale, Milne, Richard, Mount, Ian, & Wise, Peter (2018, September 20). Who Went to Jail for Their Role in the Financial Crisis? *The Financial Times*. Retrieved from https://ig.ft.com/jailed-bankers
9 Crotty (2009).
10 Ashcraft, Adam B., Goldsmith-Pinkham, Paul, & Vickery, James I. (2010). MBS Ratings and the Mortgage Credit Boom. *SSRN Electronic Journal*. Retrieved from www.newyorkfed.org/medialibrary/media/research/staff_reports/sr449.pdf
11 Minsky, H. P. (1999). The Financial Instability Hypothesis. Levy Economic Institute of Bard College. *Working Paper No.* 74. Retrieved from www.levyinstitute.org/pubs/wp74.pdf
12 Crotty, J. (2009). The Bonus-Driven "Rainmaker" Financial Firm: How These Firms Enrich Top Employees, Destroy Shareholder Value and Create System Financial Instability. *Economics Department Working Paper Series. 2*. Retrieved from www.umass.edu/economics/publications/2009-13.pdf
13 Hu, Da-Wai, Huntington, David, Mi, Frances, Frey, Manuel, Bergman, Mark, Hirsh, Robert, & Weiss, Paul (2010, July 7). Summary of Dodd-Frank Financial Regulation Legislation. Retrieved from https://corpgov.law.harvard.edu/2010/07/07/summary-of-dodd-frank-financial-regulation-legislation/
14 Keynes, J. M. (1936). *The General Theory of Employment, Interest, and Money* (First edition). New York: Harcourt, Brace & World, p. 154.
15 Let Wall Street Pay for the Restoration of Main Street Act (2009). H.R.4191, 111th Congress.
16 www.robinhoodtax.org/faq/
17 Wall Street Fair Share Act (2009). S.2927, 111th Congress.
18 Wall Street Trading and Speculators Tax Act (2011). S.1787, 112th Congress.
19 Wall Street Trading and Speculators Tax Act (2013). S.410, 113th Congress
20 Wall Street Tax Act of 2019 (2019). S.647, 116th Congress.
21 Wall Street Tax Act of 2019 (2019). H.R.1516, 116th Congress.
22 Free College, Cancel Debt (n.d.). Bernie Sanders Official Campaign Website. Retrieved from https://berniesanders.com/issues/free-college-cancel-debt/
23 At the macro level, the idea that these would be "free" is ridiculous.
24 NASCAR does have plenty of rules in place so that no one team has access to superior technology to ensure a fair playing field.
25 US Census Bureau, Real Median Household Income in the United States [MEHOINUSA672N]. Retrieved from FRED, Federal Reserve Bank of St. Louis; https://fred.stlouisfed.org/series/MEHOINUSA672N (accessed April 15, 2020).
26 Author's calculation assuming a married couple filing jointly without dependents or retirement contributions. Retrieved from www.nerdwallet.com/taxes/tax-calculator.
27 This household could contribute pretax money to an IRA or 401k. However, this assumes that the household is saving for retirement or they be forced to pay early-withdrawal penalties.
28 Ultra-Millionaire Tax (n.d.). Elizabeth Warren Official Campaign Website. Retrieved from https://elizabethwarren.com/plans/ultra-millionaire-tax
29 Tax on Extreme Wealth (n.d.). Bernie Sanders Official Campaign Website. Retrieved from https://berniesanders.com/issues/tax-extreme-wealth/
30 Hirschkorn, Phil (1999, November 9). Trump Proposes Massive One-time Tax on the Rich. *CNN.com*. Retrieved from www.cnn.com/ALLPOLITICS/stories/1999/11/09/trump.rich/index.html

31 US Department of the Treasury. Fiscal Service, Federal Debt: Total Public Debt [GFDEBTN]. Retrieved from FRED, Federal Reserve Bank of St. Louis; https://fred.stlouisfed.org/series/GFDEBTN (accessed April 13, 2020).
32 Evolution of Wealth Indicators, USA, 1913–2014 (n.d.). World Inequality Database. Retrieved from https://wid.world/share/#0/countrytimeseries/ahweal_p99p100_992_t;ahweal_p99.91p100_z;ahweal_p99p100_z/US/2015/kk/k/x/yearly/a/false/0/80000000/curve/false/1913/2014
33 Schneider, Howard, & Kahn, Chris (2020, January 10). Majority of Americans Favor Wealth Tax on Very Rich: Reuters/Ipsos Poll. *Reuters*. Retrieved from www.reuters.com/article/us-usa-election-inequality-poll-idUSKBN1Z9141
34 Of course, large amounts of wealth can be used to rent-seek.
35 Bricker, Jesse, Dettling, Lisa J., Henriques, Alice, Hsu, Joanne W., Jacobs, Lindsay, Pack, Sarah, Sabelhaus, John, & Thompson, Jeffrey (2017). Changes in U.S. Family Finances from 2013 to 2016: Evidence from the Survey of Consumer Finances. *Federal Reserve Bulletin*, *103*(3).
36 Desjardins, Jeff (2018, January 19). *Chart: What Assets Make Up Wealth?* Visual Capitalist. Retrieved from www.visualcapitalist.com/chart-assets-make-wealth/
37 The Fed – Chart: Balance Sheet of Households and Nonprofit Organizations, 1952–2019. (2020, March 12). Retrieved from www.federalreserve.gov/releases/z1/dataviz/z1/balance_sheet/chart/
38 Eisinger, Jesse, & Kiel, Paul (2019, April 5). Gutting the IRS: The IRS Tried to Take on the Ultrawealthy. It Didn't Go Well. *ProPublica*. Retrieved from www.propublica.org/article/ultrawealthy-taxes-irs-internal-revenue-service-global-high-wealth-audits
39 Saez, Emmanuel, & Zucman, Gabriel (2019). *The Triumph of Injustice: How the Rich Dodge Taxes and How to Make Them Pay* (First edition). New York: W. W. Norton & Company.
40 For that story, read the Saez and Zucman book.
41 Mazzoleni, Roberto, & Nelson, Richard R. (1998). The Benefits and Costs of Strong Patent Protection: A Contribution to the Current Debate. *Research Policy*, *27*(3), 273–284.
42 Moser, Petra (2013). Patents and Innovation: Evidence from Economic History. *Journal of Economic Perspectives*, *27*(1), 23–44.
43 Romer, P. M. (1990) Endogenous Technological Change. *Journal of Political Economy*, *98*, 71–102.
44 Jones, Charles I. (1995). R & D-Based Models of Economic Growth. *Journal of Political Economy*, *103*(4), 759–784.
45 STRONGER Patents Act of 2019 (2019). H.R.3666, 116th Congress. Retrieved from www.congress.gov/bill/116th-congress/house-bill/3666/text
46 STRONGER Patents Act of 2019 (2019).
47 Boldrin, M., & Levine, D. K. (2012). The Case Against Patents. *Federal Reserve Bank of St. Louis Working Paper Series, Working Paper* 2012–035A, p. 1. Retrieved from https://files.stlouisfed.org/files/htdocs/wp/2012/2012-035.pdf
48 There is evidence from China that incentivizing the production of patents leads to a decrease in patent quality. It should be noted, however, that the mechanism in China involves tax incentives and subsidies to patent owners. Long, Cheryl X., & Wang, Jun (2018). China's Patent Promotion Policies and Its Quality Implications. *Science and Public Policy*, *46*, 91–104.

49 FDA (2020, March 24). FDA Approves First Generic of Daraprim. Retrieved from www.fda.gov/news-events/press-announcements/fda-approves-first-generic-daraprim

50 Pollack, Andrew (2015, September 20). Drug Goes From $13.50 a Tablet to $750, Overnight. *The New York Times*. Retrieved from www.nytimes.com/2015/09/21/business/a-huge-overnight-increase-in-a-drugs-price-raises-protests.html

51 NICE Citizens Council (2004, November). Citizens Council Report: Ultra Orphan Drugs. Retrieved from www.nice.org.uk/Media/Default/Get-involved/Citizens-Council/Reports/CCReport04UltraOrphanDrugs.pdf

52 Boldrin & Levine (2012).

# Index

Note: Page numbers in *italics* indicate a figure and page numbers in **bold** indicate a table on the corresponding page.